# Summer Bridge Math
## Grades 2–3

**Editor: Sandra Toland**
**Layout Design: Tiara Reynolds**
**Inside Illustrations: Nathan Aaron, Mike Duggins, Ray Lambert, Wayne Miller**
**Cover Design: Chasity Rice**
**Cover Illustration: Wayne Miller**

ISBN 978-1-60022-451-5

# Table of Contents

# How to Use This Book

The *Summer Bridge Math* series is designed to help children improve their mathematical skills during the summer months and between grades. *Summer Bridge Math* includes several extra components to help make your child's study of mathematics easier and more inviting.

For example, an **Assessment** test has been included to help you determine your child's mathematical knowledge and what skills need improvement. Use this test, as well as the **Assessment Analysis**, as a diagnostic tool for those areas in which your child may need extra practice.

Furthermore, the **Incentive Contract** will motivate your child to complete the work in *Summer Bridge Math*. Together, you and your child choose the reward for completing specific sections of the book. Check off the pages that your child has completed, and he or she will have a record of his or her accomplishment.

**Examples** are included for each new skill that your child will learn. The examples are located in red boxes at the top of the pages. On each page, the directions refer to the example your child needs to complete a specific type of activity.

# Assessment

**Write each numeral.**

**A.** seven _____      nineteen _____      thirty-seven _____

seventy _____      sixty-five _____

**What is the value of:**

**B.** 6 in 612? _____      4 in 241? _____      9 in 9,243? _____

**C.** 342 equals _____ hundreds _____ tens _____ ones

**D.** 819 equals _____ hundreds _____ tens _____ ones

**E.** 2,345 equals _____ thousands _____ hundreds _____ tens _____ ones

**Use <, >, or = to compare the numerals.**

**F.** 35 _____ 71      10 _____ 3      91 _____ 94      68 _____ 88

**Solve the problems.**

**G.**

| 21 | 64 | 86 | 59 | 73 |
|---|---|---|---|---|
| + 42 | + 12 | + 11 | + 19 | + 17 |

**H.**

| 49 | 83 | 77 | 40 | 54 |
|---|---|---|---|---|
| − 37 | − 13 | − 41 | − 16 | − 27 |

**I.**

| 12 | 7 | 79 | 8 | 32 |
|---|---|---|---|---|
| x 2 | x 6 | x 7 | x 2 | x 8 |

**J.** 7)49      5)35      4)28      6)38      8)25

     **Summer Bridge Math** RB-904087

# Assessment (continued)

**Write the equations for each fact family.**

**K.** 2, 4, 8

_____ X _____ = _____
_____ X _____ = _____
_____ ÷ _____ = _____
_____ ÷ _____ = _____

**L.** 5, 6, 30

_____ X _____ = _____
_____ X _____ = _____
_____ ÷ _____ = _____
_____ ÷ _____ = _____

**Write the time shown on each clock.**

**M.**

____ : ____        ____ : ____

**Count the money. Write how much.**

**N.**

_____

**Write the fractions. Then, use <, >, or = to compare.**

**O.**

_____    _____

**P.**

_____    _____

**Write the name of each shape.**

**Q.**

_____   _____   _____   _____

**Solve each problem.**

**R.** The soccer team scored 6 goals each game. They played 3 games. How many goals did they score? _____ goals

**S.** Sam's family has 12 cookies. There are 4 people in Sam's family. How many cookies will each person get? _____ cookies

 **Summer Bridge Math** RB-904087

© Rainbow Bridge Publishing

# Assessment Analysis

After reviewing the Assessment test, match the problems answered incorrectly to the corresponding activity pages. Your child should spend extra time on those activities to strengthen his or her math skills.

| Diagnostic Problem | Review Section | Review Pages |
|---|---|---|
| A., B., C., D., E., F. | Numeration | 7–18 |
| G., H. | Addition & Subtraction | 19–34 |
| I., J., K., L. | Multiplication & Division | 35–51 |
| M., N. | Time & Money | 52–58 |
| O., P. | Fractions & Decimals | 63–73 |
| Q. | Geometry | 74–80 |
| R., S. | Problem Solving | 84–92 |

© Rainbow Bridge Publishing    **Summer Bridge Math** RB-904087

# Incentive Contract

| Numeration | | √ | My Incentive Is: |
|---|---|---|---|
| 7 | Naming Numbers in Word Form | | |
| 8 | Naming Larger Numbers in Word Form | | |
| 9 | Reading Number Words Practice | | |
| 10 | Ordinal Numbers | | |
| 11 | Place Value | | |
| 12 | Place Value Practice | | |
| 13 | Writing in Expanded Form | | |
| 14 | Writing in Standard Form | | |
| 15 | Comparing the Values of Numerals | | |
| 16 | Comparing Numerals Practice | | |
| 17 | Rounding to the Nearest Hundred | | |
| 18 | Skip Counting | | |

| Addition | | √ | My Incentive Is: |
|---|---|---|---|
| 19 | Two-Digit Addition | | |
| 20 | Two-Digit Addition with Regrouping | | |
| 21 | Three-Digit Addition | | |
| 22 | Three-Digit Addition with Regrouping | | |
| 23 | Four-Digit Addition | | |
| 24 | Column Addition | | |
| 25 | Adding Money | | |

| Subtraction | | √ | My Incentive Is: |
|---|---|---|---|
| 26 | Two-Digit Subtraction | | |
| 27 | Two-Digit Subtraction with Regrouping | | |
| 28 | Three-Digit Subtraction | | |
| 29 | Three-Digit Subtraction with Regrouping | | |
| 30 | Four-Digit Subtraction | | |
| 31 | Subtraction with Regrouping Practice | | |

| Mixed Addition and Subtraction | | √ | My Incentive Is: |
|---|---|---|---|
| 32 | Two-Digit Mixed Practice | | |
| 33 | Three-Digit Mixed Practice | | |
| 34 | Out of This World! | | |

| Multiplication | | √ | My Incentive Is: |
|---|---|---|---|
| 35 | Introduction to Multiplication | | |
| 36 | Multiplication Chart | | |
| 37 | Finding the Facts | | |
| 38 | Multiplication Practice | | |
| 39 | Two-Digit Multiplication | | |
| 40 | Two-Digit Multiplication with Regrouping | | |
| 41 | Three-Digit Multiplication | | |
| 42 | Multiplying Money | | |

| Division | | √ | My Incentive Is: |
|---|---|---|---|
| 43 | Introduction to Division | | |
| 44 | Understanding Division | | |
| 45 | Using Division Signs | | |
| 46 | Dividing by a Single-Digit Numeral | | |
| 47 | Division with Remainders | | |
| 48 | Division Practice | | |

| Mixed Multiplication and Division | | √ | My Incentive Is: |
|---|---|---|---|
| 49 | Connecting Operations | | |
| 50 | Fact Families | | |
| 51 | Mixed Practice | | |

| Time and Money | | √ | My Incentive Is: |
|---|---|---|---|
| 52 | Telling Time | | |
| 53 | Five-Minute Intervals | | |
| 54 | Drawing Hands on Clocks | | |
| 55 | Introduction to Money | | |
| 56 | Skip Counting Coins | | |
| 57 | Counting Money | | |
| 58 | Calculating Change | | |

| Measurement | | √ | My Incentive Is: |
|---|---|---|---|
| 59 | Standard Measurement | | |
| 60 | Comparing Linear Measurements | | |
| 61 | Increments and Weight | | |
| 62 | Capacity and Temperature | | |

| Fractions and Decimals | | √ | My Incentive Is: |
|---|---|---|---|
| 63 | Introduction to Fractions | | |
| 64 | Equivalent Fractions | | |
| 65 | Comparing Fractions | | |
| 66 | Adding and Subtracting Fractions | | |
| 67 | Improper Fractions | | |
| 68 | Sequencing Decimals | | |
| 69 | Using Decimals | | |
| 70 | Adding and Subtracting Decimals | | |
| 71 | Tenths | | |
| 72 | Tenths Practice | | |
| 73 | Place Value Practice | | |

| Patterns and Geometry | | √ | My Incentive Is: |
|---|---|---|---|
| 74 | Predicting Patterns | | |
| 75 | Number Patterns | | |
| 76 | Patterns and Functions | | |
| 77 | Shapes | | |
| 78 | Spatial Figures | | |
| 79 | Lines of Symmetry | | |
| 80 | Perimeter | | |

| Statistics and Graphs | | √ | My Incentive Is: |
|---|---|---|---|
| 81 | Exploring Probability | | |
| 82 | Reading a Chart | | |
| 83 | Interpreting Graphs and Grids | | |

| Problem Solving | | √ | My Incentive Is: |
|---|---|---|---|
| 84 | Addition and Subtraction | | |
| 85 | Three-Digit Addition and Subtraction | | |
| 86 | Multiplication | | |
| 87 | Choosing the Operation | | |
| 88 | Division | | |
| 89 | Division with Remainders | | |
| 90 | Time | | |
| 91 | Money | | |
| 92 | Problem Solving Using Charts | | |

# Naming Numbers in Word Form

> **Numbers** can be written as words, as well as numerals. Below are the words for the numerals 0 through 12.
>
> | 0–zero | 1–one | 2–two | 3–three | 4–four |
> |--------|-------|-------|---------|--------|
> | 5–five | 6–six | 7–seven | 8–eight | 9–nine |
> | 10–ten | 11–eleven | 12–twelve | | |

**Study the word names above. Then, find the written name for each numeral. Use the matching letters to answer the question.**

**Where does the male emperor penguin keep the eggs warm?**

$$\overline{\phantom{X}}\ \ \overline{\phantom{X}} \qquad\qquad \overline{\phantom{X}}\ \ \overline{\phantom{X}}\ \ \overline{\phantom{X}}$$
74    19          46    93    36

$$\overline{\phantom{X}}\ \ \overline{\phantom{X}}\ \ \overline{\phantom{X}}\ \ \overline{\phantom{X}}\ \ \overline{\phantom{X}}$$
21    52    76    62    85

| | | | | | |
|---|---|---|---|---|---|
| ninety-three | I | sixty-two | T | forty-six | H |
| fifty-nine | R | seventy-four | O | fifty-two | E |
| nineteen | N | eighty-five | ! | twenty-one | F |
| seventy-six | E | thirty-six | S | ninety | V |

**Summer Bridge Math** RB-904087

# Naming Larger Numbers in Word Form

You can use **place value** columns to help you write numbers in word form. They look like this:

| H | T | O |
|---|---|---|
| 6 | 4 | 1 |

= six hundred forty-one

| Th | H | T | O |
|----|---|---|---|
| 3 | 2 | 1 | 8 |

= three thousand two hundred eighteen

**Study the examples above. Then, read each number's name in word form. Color its matching number on the chicken or on the egg.**

**A.** six thousand nine hundred eleven

**B.** four thousand seventy-three

**C.** nine thousand two hundred seven

**D.** eight hundred thirty-nine

**E.** nine thousand six hundred one

**F.** eight thousand three hundred ninety

**G.** four hundred seventeen

**H.** five thousand eighty-two

**I.** four hundred seventy

**J.** three thousand five hundred twelve

**K.** six thousand nine hundred fourteen

417    9,207    839

3,512    6,911    6,914

9,601    4,073    5,082

470    4,413    8,390

**L.** What numeral is left over? _____

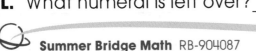

Summer Bridge Math RB-904087          © Rainbow Bridge Publishing

# Reading Number Words Practice

This number is **seven hundred forty-three**. Do not use the word "and" when writing or saying large numbers.

**743**

**Study the examples on page 8. Then, draw lines to match the numeral with the number words.**

| | | |
|---|---|---|
| **A.** | 347 | five hundred nine |
| **B.** | 279 | nine hundred ninety-nine |
| **C.** | 960 | three hundred forty-seven |
| **D.** | 719 | nine hundred sixty |
| **E.** | 801 | one hundred thirty-five |
| **F.** | 590 | six hundred eighty |
| **G.** | 135 | two hundred seventy-nine |
| **H.** | 509 | seven hundred nineteen |
| **I.** | 680 | eight hundred one |
| **J.** | 999 | five hundred ninety |

**Write the numeral that means the same as each number word.**

**K.** three hundred thirteen _____

**L.** eight hundred nine _____

**M.** four hundred twenty-six _____

**N.** two hundred eleven _____

**O.** seven hundred fifty-one _____

**P.** one hundred five _____

**Q.** five hundred thirty-two _____

**R.** nine hundred forty-four _____

**Summer Bridge Math** RB-904087

# Ordinal Numbers

The **ordinal** of an object is found by counting its place in line. To count ordinal numbers, use first (1st), second (2nd), third (3rd), etc.

**Write the missing numbers on the tickets to show their order. Then, use the tickets to help you find the answers to the questions.**

A. 1st 2nd 3rd 4th

B. 18th 19th 20th 25th

C. 79th 83rd 88th

D. If you are holding the eighth ticket, how many people are ahead of you? _____

E. You are 14th out of 19 people in line. How many people are behind you? _____

F. You are 11th and your friend is 13th. Which place is the person between you? _____

Summer Bridge Math RB-904087

# Place Value

I thousand, 2 hundreds, 3 tens, 2 ones
is equal to the number 1,232. We say
"one thousand two hundred thirty-two."

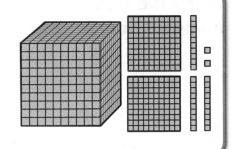

___1___ thousand ___2___ hundreds ___3___ tens
___2___ ones = ___1,232___

**Study the example above. Then, write how many thousands, hundreds, tens, and ones. Write the total.**

**A.**

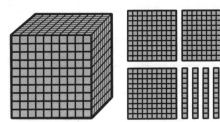

_____ thousands _____ hundreds
_____ tens _____ ones = _____

**B.**

_____ thousands _____ hundreds
_____ tens _____ ones = _____

**C.**

_____ thousands _____ hundreds
_____ tens _____ ones = _____

**D.**

_____ thousands _____ hundreds
_____ tens _____ ones = _____

**E.**

_____ thousands _____ hundreds
_____ tens _____ ones = _____

**F.**

_____ thousands _____ hundreds
_____ tens _____ ones = _____

**Summer Bridge Math** RB-904087

# Place Value Practice

**Study the example on page 11. Then, write the value of each numeral below.**

| | Ten Thousands | Thousands | Hundreds | Tens | Ones |
|---|---|---|---|---|---|
| | | | | | |
| | | | | | |
| | | | | | |
| | | | | | |
| | | | | | |
| | | | | | |
| | | | | | |
| | | | | | |
| | | | | | |
| | | | | | |
| | | | | | |
| | | | | | |
| | | | | | |
| | | | | | |

**A.** 5,739

**B.** 14,650

**C.** 27,381

**D.** 40,736

**E.** 91,475

**F.** 55,837

**G.** 86,902

**H.** 4,560

**I.** 31,048

**J.** 11,111

**K.** 79,277

**L.** 68,593

**M.** 99,999

**N.** 48,305

## What place value does each circled numeral represent?

**O.** 3,④56 _____     90,②86 _____

**P.** ⑦,394 _____     ④7,519 _____

**Q.** ①6,321 _____     38,1②7 _____

**R.** 25,0④7 _____     ⑧4,031 _____

**S.** 39,⑤86 _____     7②,797 _____

**T.** 58,72⑨ _____     59,3⑥8 _____

**U.** 40,3⑦0 _____     30,58④ _____

**V.** ⑦2,532 _____     ⑧6,395 _____

**W.** 9⑥,411 _____     39,⑤86 _____

**Summer Bridge Math** RB-904087    

# Writing in Expanded Form

The place value system is based on **groups of ten**. This chart shows how the thousands, hundreds, tens, and ones relate to each other.

| 1,000 | 100 | 10 | 1 |
|---|---|---|---|
| 1 thousand = 10 hundreds | 1 hundred = 10 tens | 1 ten = 10 ones | |

This chart is helpful when writing numbers in expanded form.

$$3,649 = 3,000 + 600 + 40 + 9$$

**Study the example above. Then, write each number in expanded form.**

| | | | 1,000 | 100 | 10 | 1 |
|---|---|---|---|---|---|---|
| A. | 9,516 | = | | + | + | + |
| B. | 2,358 | = | | + | + | + |
| C. | 1,407 | = | | + | + | + |
| D. | 921 | = | | + | + | + |
| E. | 7,800 | = | | + | + | + |
| F. | 3,264 | = | | + | + | + |
| G. | 5,182 | = | | + | + | + |
| H. | 614 | = | | + | + | + |
| I. | 4,073 | = | | + | + | + |
| J. | 9,530 | = | | + | + | + |

**Summer Bridge Math** RB-904087

# Writing in Standard Form

**Study the example on page 13. Then, write the numeral that means the same as each expanded number.**

**A.**  1,000 + 500 + 30 + 3 =  _____

**B.**  5,000 + 900 + 40 + 7 =  _____

**C.**  3,000 + 700 + 50 + 5 =  _____

**D.**  7,000 + 400 + 70 + 9 =  _____

**E.**  9,000 + 20 + 1 =  _____

**F.**  3,000 + 100 + 2 =  _____

**G.**  3,000 + 500 + 6 =  _____

**H.**  6,000 + 90 + 8 =  _____

**I.**  3,000 + 600 + 9 =  _____

**J.**  1,000 + 600 + 90 + 8 =  _____

## Write the number in expanded form.

**K.**  3,456 _____

**L.**  7,324 _____

**M.**  9,152 _____

**N.**  3,569 _____

**O.**  2,431 _____

**P.**  4,022 _____

# Comparing the Values of Numerals

The arrow points to the smaller number and opens wide to the larger number. 64 > 62 means that 64 is **greater than** 62.

    <

| = | > | < |
|---|---|---|
| means<br>equal to | means<br>greater than | means<br>less than |

**Study the example above. Then, use >, <, or = to compare each set of numerals.**

A.        72        [   ]        27

B.        61        [   ]        60

C.        34        [   ]        43

D.        27        [   ]        27

E.        23        [   ]        32

F.        98        [   ]        96

G.        82        [   ]        83

H.        56        [   ]        65

I.        18        [   ]        18

J.        49        [   ]        50

**Summer Bridge Math** RB-904087

# Comparing Numerals Practice

**Circle the numeral that is the least.**

| | | | | | | |
|---|---|---|---|---|---|---|
| **A.** | 173 | 149 | 156 | 206 | 347 | 165 |
| **B.** | 699 | 943 | 943 | 878 | 566 | 903 |
| **C.** | 510 | 430 | 530 | 770 | 680 | 820 |
| **D.** | 390 | 745 | 845 | 691 | 759 | 425 |
| **E.** | 941 | 812 | 852 | 814 | 916 | 804 |

**Circle the numeral that is the most.**

| | | | | | | |
|---|---|---|---|---|---|---|
| **F.** | 746 | 981 | 873 | 699 | 870 | 847 |
| **G.** | 633 | 709 | 599 | 671 | 433 | 598 |
| **H.** | 695 | 768 | 845 | 871 | 555 | 796 |
| **I.** | 493 | 561 | 664 | 793 | 990 | 889 |
| **J.** | 567 | 765 | 675 | 783 | 623 | 805 |

**Use greater than (>) and less than (<) signs to compare numerals.**

**K.** 439 _____ 670            944 _____ 872

**L.** 730 _____ 750            610 _____ 603

**M.** 567 _____ 576            887 _____ 891

**N.** 991 _____ 919            499 _____ 500

**O.** 635 _____ 471            781 _____ 902

**P.** 1000 _____ 998           549 _____ 798

**Q.** 473 _____ 374            895 _____ 958

**R.** 768 _____ 391            399 _____ 405

**S.** 818 _____ 881            914 _____ 941

# Rounding to the Nearest Hundred

When **rounding** to the nearest hundred, use these rules:
1. Look at the tens place.
2. If the number in the tens place is 0, 1, 2, 3, or 4, round down.
3. If the number in the tens place is 5, 6, 7, 8, or 9, round up.

**You have discovered a hidden treasure! Study the rules above for rounding. Then, estimate the value in each treasure chest. Round these amounts to the nearest hundred.**

$692  $700

$140  $

$569  $

$303  $

$684  $

$851  $

$712  $

$476  $

$925  $

17

**Summer Bridge Math** RB-904087

# Skip Counting

**Skip counting** means following a given pattern as you count. You are probably used to counting by twos, fives, and tens. Use the number line to "skip" the given number of times.

Count by fives.

## Study the example above. Then, color the number boxes to show skip counting.

**A.** Start at 0 and count by fours.

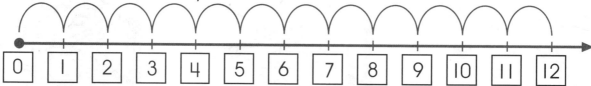

**B.** Start at 0 and count by sixes.

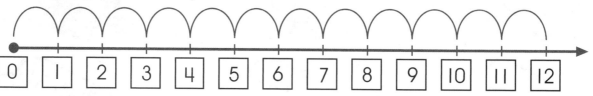

**C.** Start at 33 and count by threes.

**D.** Start at 62 and count by twos.

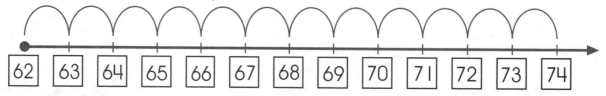

**E.** Start at 84 and count by fours.

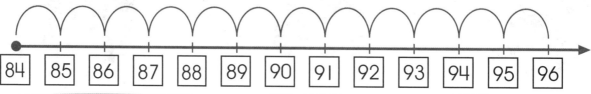

**Summer Bridge Math** RB-904087

# Two-Digit Addition

| 1. Add the ones column. Five plus 3 equals 8. | 2. Add the tens column. Two plus 1 equals 3. |
|---|---|
| $\begin{array}{r} 2\mathbf{5} \\ +\ 1\mathbf{3} \\ \hline \mathbf{8} \end{array}$ | $\begin{array}{r} \mathbf{2}5 \\ +\ \mathbf{1}3 \\ \hline \mathbf{3}8 \end{array}$ |

## Study the example above. Then, solve each problem.

**A.**

| 23 | 64 | 47 | 13 | 55 | 16 |
|---|---|---|---|---|---|
| + 42 | + 25 | + 31 | + 45 | + 30 | + 53 |

**B.**

| 70 | 82 | 74 | 58 | 26 | 35 |
|---|---|---|---|---|---|
| + 29 | + 11 | + 23 | + 41 | + 33 | + 54 |

**C.**

| 12 | 83 | 41 | 19 | 22 | 36 |
|---|---|---|---|---|---|
| + 77 | + 13 | + 37 | + 60 | + 37 | + 23 |

**D.**

| 15 | 18 | 84 | 27 | 46 | 20 |
|---|---|---|---|---|---|
| + 72 | + 81 | + 12 | + 62 | + 41 | + 51 |

**E.**

| 52 | 75 | 24 | 51 | 29 | 25 |
|---|---|---|---|---|---|
| + 36 | + 10 | + 43 | + 27 | + 50 | + 61 |

**F.**

| 31 | 47 | 19 | 62 | 33 | 43 |
|---|---|---|---|---|---|
| + 55 | + 32 | + 30 | + 37 | + 52 | + 31 |

| 1. Add the ones column. Eight plus 4 equals 12. **Regroup** the tens column. | 2. Add the tens column. Six plus 2 plus 1 equals 9. |
|---|---|
| $$\begin{array}{r} 1\phantom{0} \\ 6\,\mathbf{8} \\ +\ 2\,\mathbf{4} \\ \hline \mathbf{2} \end{array}$$ | $$\begin{array}{r} 1\phantom{0} \\ \mathbf{6}\,8 \\ +\ \mathbf{2}\,4 \\ \hline \mathbf{9}\,2 \end{array}$$ |

## Study the example above. Then, solve each problem.

**A.**

$$\begin{array}{r} 27 \\ +\ 24 \\ \hline \end{array} \qquad \begin{array}{r} 39 \\ +\ 53 \\ \hline \end{array} \qquad \begin{array}{r} 46 \\ +\ 35 \\ \hline \end{array} \qquad \begin{array}{r} 57 \\ +\ 29 \\ \hline \end{array} \qquad \begin{array}{r} 49 \\ +\ 15 \\ \hline \end{array} \qquad \begin{array}{r} 63 \\ +\ 27 \\ \hline \end{array}$$

**B.**

$$\begin{array}{r} 75 \\ +\ 19 \\ \hline \end{array} \qquad \begin{array}{r} 93 \\ +\ 37 \\ \hline \end{array} \qquad \begin{array}{r} 58 \\ +\ 34 \\ \hline \end{array} \qquad \begin{array}{r} 64 \\ +\ 28 \\ \hline \end{array} \qquad \begin{array}{r} 86 \\ +\ 17 \\ \hline \end{array} \qquad \begin{array}{r} 47 \\ +\ 28 \\ \hline \end{array}$$

**C.**

$$\begin{array}{r} 66 \\ +\ 26 \\ \hline \end{array} \qquad \begin{array}{r} 79 \\ +\ 32 \\ \hline \end{array} \qquad \begin{array}{r} 43 \\ +\ 27 \\ \hline \end{array} \qquad \begin{array}{r} 56 \\ +\ 58 \\ \hline \end{array} \qquad \begin{array}{r} 98 \\ +\ 32 \\ \hline \end{array} \qquad \begin{array}{r} 81 \\ +\ 59 \\ \hline \end{array}$$

**D.**

$$\begin{array}{r} 64 \\ +\ 17 \\ \hline \end{array} \qquad \begin{array}{r} 57 \\ +\ 26 \\ \hline \end{array} \qquad \begin{array}{r} 34 \\ +\ 49 \\ \hline \end{array} \qquad \begin{array}{r} 25 \\ +\ 36 \\ \hline \end{array} \qquad \begin{array}{r} 18 \\ +\ 28 \\ \hline \end{array} \qquad \begin{array}{r} 27 \\ +\ 59 \\ \hline \end{array}$$

**E.**

$$\begin{array}{r} 43 \\ +\ 27 \\ \hline \end{array} \qquad \begin{array}{r} 26 \\ +\ 36 \\ \hline \end{array} \qquad \begin{array}{r} 27 \\ +\ 69 \\ \hline \end{array} \qquad \begin{array}{r} 53 \\ +\ 37 \\ \hline \end{array} \qquad \begin{array}{r} 33 \\ +\ 48 \\ \hline \end{array} \qquad \begin{array}{r} 49 \\ +\ 27 \\ \hline \end{array}$$

*Summer Bridge Math* RB-904087

# Three-Digit Addition

| 1. Add the ones column. Two plus 4 equals 6. | 2. Add the tens column. Six plus 3 equals 9. | 3. Add the hundreds column. Four plus 1 equals 5. |
|---|---|---|
| $\begin{array}{r} 46\textbf{2} \\ +13\textbf{4} \\ \hline \textbf{6} \end{array}$ | $\begin{array}{r} 4\textbf{6}2 \\ +1\textbf{3}4 \\ \hline \textbf{9}6 \end{array}$ | $\begin{array}{r} \textbf{4}62 \\ +\textbf{1}34 \\ \hline \textbf{5}96 \end{array}$ |

**Study the example above. Then, solve each problem.**

**A.**
$\begin{array}{r} 182 \\ +703 \\ \hline \end{array}$
$\begin{array}{r} 231 \\ +547 \\ \hline \end{array}$
$\begin{array}{r} 825 \\ +163 \\ \hline \end{array}$
$\begin{array}{r} 436 \\ +562 \\ \hline \end{array}$
$\begin{array}{r} 325 \\ +202 \\ \hline \end{array}$

**B.**
$\begin{array}{r} 274 \\ +320 \\ \hline \end{array}$
$\begin{array}{r} 641 \\ +345 \\ \hline \end{array}$
$\begin{array}{r} 908 \\ +\ 61 \\ \hline \end{array}$
$\begin{array}{r} 365 \\ +424 \\ \hline \end{array}$
$\begin{array}{r} 207 \\ +712 \\ \hline \end{array}$

**C.**
$\begin{array}{r} 352 \\ +436 \\ \hline \end{array}$
$\begin{array}{r} 475 \\ +510 \\ \hline \end{array}$
$\begin{array}{r} 724 \\ +143 \\ \hline \end{array}$
$\begin{array}{r} 650 \\ +227 \\ \hline \end{array}$
$\begin{array}{r} 298 \\ +500 \\ \hline \end{array}$

**D.**
$\begin{array}{r} 525 \\ +261 \\ \hline \end{array}$
$\begin{array}{r} 631 \\ +155 \\ \hline \end{array}$
$\begin{array}{r} 447 \\ +432 \\ \hline \end{array}$
$\begin{array}{r} 319 \\ +450 \\ \hline \end{array}$
$\begin{array}{r} 752 \\ +136 \\ \hline \end{array}$

**E.**
$\begin{array}{r} 933 \\ +\ 52 \\ \hline \end{array}$
$\begin{array}{r} 547 \\ +131 \\ \hline \end{array}$
$\begin{array}{r} 830 \\ +\ 69 \\ \hline \end{array}$
$\begin{array}{r} 626 \\ +331 \\ \hline \end{array}$
$\begin{array}{r} 487 \\ +411 \\ \hline \end{array}$

**F.**
$\begin{array}{r} 631 \\ +325 \\ \hline \end{array}$
$\begin{array}{r} 488 \\ +211 \\ \hline \end{array}$
$\begin{array}{r} 562 \\ +407 \\ \hline \end{array}$
$\begin{array}{r} 723 \\ +166 \\ \hline \end{array}$
$\begin{array}{r} 506 \\ +353 \\ \hline \end{array}$

**Summer Bridge Math** RB-904087

# Three-Digit Addition with Regrouping

Once you know how to add 3-digit numbers, you can add any size numbers together. Remember: always start with the ones column and work your way through the columns to the left.

**Study the example on page 20. Then, solve each problem.**

**A.**

$$
\begin{array}{r} 283 \\ + 168 \end{array}
\qquad
\begin{array}{r} 497 \\ + 205 \end{array}
\qquad
\begin{array}{r} 176 \\ + 640 \end{array}
\qquad
\begin{array}{r} 325 \\ + 867 \end{array}
\qquad
\begin{array}{r} 651 \\ + 179 \end{array}
$$

**B.**

$$
\begin{array}{r} 304 \\ + 519 \end{array}
\qquad
\begin{array}{r} 517 \\ + 334 \end{array}
\qquad
\begin{array}{r} 237 \\ + 807 \end{array}
\qquad
\begin{array}{r} 482 \\ + 531 \end{array}
\qquad
\begin{array}{r} 117 \\ + 488 \end{array}
$$

**C.**

$$
\begin{array}{r} 624 \\ + 276 \end{array}
\qquad
\begin{array}{r} 431 \\ + 382 \end{array}
\qquad
\begin{array}{r} 329 \\ + 682 \end{array}
\qquad
\begin{array}{r} 772 \\ + 405 \end{array}
\qquad
\begin{array}{r} 532 \\ + 489 \end{array}
$$

**D.**

$$
\begin{array}{r} 136 \\ + 477 \end{array}
\qquad
\begin{array}{r} 479 \\ + 342 \end{array}
\qquad
\begin{array}{r} 379 \\ + 483 \end{array}
\qquad
\begin{array}{r} 386 \\ + 364 \end{array}
\qquad
\begin{array}{r} 670 \\ + 259 \end{array}
$$

**E.**

$$
\begin{array}{r} 823 \\ + 357 \end{array}
\qquad
\begin{array}{r} 937 \\ + 468 \end{array}
\qquad
\begin{array}{r} 736 \\ + 136 \end{array}
\qquad
\begin{array}{r} 648 \\ + 246 \end{array}
\qquad
\begin{array}{r} 462 \\ + 369 \end{array}
$$

**F.**

$$
\begin{array}{r} 837 \\ + 337 \end{array}
\qquad
\begin{array}{r} 689 \\ + 285 \end{array}
\qquad
\begin{array}{r} 350 \\ + 261 \end{array}
\qquad
\begin{array}{r} 427 \\ + 367 \end{array}
\qquad
\begin{array}{r} 601 \\ + 289 \end{array}
$$

# Four-Digit Addition

**Study the examples on pages 19–21. Then, solve each problem.**

**A.**  
3,261  
+ 5,239

4,639  
+ 2,073

7,216  
+ 2,593

5,952  
+ 3,128

1,794  
+ 2,607

**B.**  
2,773  
+ 3,535

9,076  
+ 3,970

6,415  
+ 1,765

4,701  
+ 6,354

8,213  
+ 1,529

**C.**  
3,257  
+ 4,809

9,935  
+ 1,260

1,224  
+ 8,967

6,597  
+ 3,212

4,165  
+ 7,042

**D.**  
7,309  
+ 4,597

3,295  
+ 4,305

5,716  
+ 1,708

6,907  
+ 4,132

8,813  
+ 2,076

**E.**  
1,943  
+ 3,065

2,967  
+ 7,120

3,846  
+ 2,195

6,381  
+ 5,436

5,490  
+ 6,327

**F.**  
8,361  
+ 4,209

5,639  
+ 2,076

1,735  
+ 3,291

2,465  
+ 3,637

9,675  
+ 2,404

23

# Column Addition

First, add the first 2 numbers. Two plus 7 equals 9.
Then, add the last number. Nine plus 4 equals 13.

$$\begin{array}{r} 2 \\ 7 \\ + 4 \end{array} \longrightarrow \begin{array}{r} 9 \\ + 4 \\ \hline 13 \end{array}$$

## Study the example above. Then, solve each problem.

**A.**

| 1 | 4 | 3 | 7 | 2 | 1 | 6 |
|---|---|---|---|---|---|---|
| 3 | 2 | 4 | 1 | 8 | 9 | 5 |
| + 2 | + 1 | + 2 | + 2 | + 1 | + 1 | + 1 |

**B.**

| 3 | 3 | 7 | 4 | 2 | 5 | 3 |
|---|---|---|---|---|---|---|
| 5 | 6 | 2 | 3 | 2 | 3 | 7 |
| + 4 | + 1 | + 4 | + 7 | + 3 | + 2 | + 2 |

**C.**

| 2 | 6 | 4 | 5 | 7 | 9 | 8 |
|---|---|---|---|---|---|---|
| 8 | 4 | 4 | 5 | 7 | 4 | 7 |
| + 3 | + 3 | + 3 | + 5 | + 3 | + 1 | + 3 |

**D.**

| 5 | 4 | 2 | 7 | 8 | 6 | 3 |
|---|---|---|---|---|---|---|
| 3 | 8 | 9 | 5 | 2 | 2 | 3 |
| 4 | 2 | 1 | 3 | 5 | 2 | 4 |
| + 1 | + 1 | + 3 | + 3 | + 3 | + 8 | + 3 |

**E.**

| 3 | 4 | 9 | 6 | 7 | 8 | 1 |
|---|---|---|---|---|---|---|
| 7 | 8 | 1 | 6 | 8 | 3 | 8 |
| 5 | 2 | 5 | 3 | 1 | 0 | 2 |
| + 1 | + 3 | + 2 | + 3 | + 2 | + 2 | + 7 |

**Summer Bridge Math** RB-904087

# Adding Money

To find the sum of several numbers, use the same steps as before:
1. Add the ones column. Regroup if necessary.
2. Add the tens column. Regroup if necessary.
3. Add the hundreds column. Regroup if necessary.
4. Add the thousands column.

When adding money, be sure to include the **decimal point** and the **dollar sign** in your answer.

**Which is the richest kingdom? Study the examples on pages 20, 21, and 24. Then, solve each problem. Be sure to include the money symbols. Color the answers on the castles. The first castle to be completely shaded is in the richest kingdom!**

**A.**

| | | |
|---|---|---|
| $1.36 | $6.77 | $2.09 |
| 2.07 | 3.52 | 0.33 |
| + 3.64 | + 1.08 | + 9.81 |
| $7.07 | | |

**B.**

| | | |
|---|---|---|
| $3.07 | $0.94 | $1.46 |
| 4.12 | 8.41 | 3.72 |
| + 6.31 | + 7.18 | + 5.40 |

**C.**

| | | |
|---|---|---|
| $3.73 | $7.17 | $4.36 |
| 3.19 | 8.01 | 5.56 |
| + 6.42 | + 2.90 | + 9.12 |

**D.**

| | |
|---|---|
| $5.71 | $1.80 |
| 0.09 | 9.84 |
| + 0.83 | + 1.06 |

$13.50
$6.63
$10.58
$12.70
$13.34
$7.07

$16.53
$12.38
$11.37
$18.08
$12.23
$19.04

**Summer Bridge Math** RB-904087

# Two-Digit Subtraction

1. Subtract the ones column.
   Six minus 2 equals 4.

$$\begin{array}{r} 3\mathbf{6} \\ -\ 1\mathbf{2} \\ \hline \mathbf{4} \end{array}$$

2. Subtract the tens column.
   Three minus 1 equals 2.

$$\begin{array}{r} \mathbf{3}6 \\ -\ \mathbf{1}2 \\ \hline \mathbf{2}4 \end{array}$$

**Study the example above. Then, solve each problem.**

**A.**
$$\begin{array}{r} 86 \\ -32 \\ \hline \end{array}$$
$$\begin{array}{r} 52 \\ -12 \\ \hline \end{array}$$
$$\begin{array}{r} 67 \\ -45 \\ \hline \end{array}$$
$$\begin{array}{r} 95 \\ -30 \\ \hline \end{array}$$
$$\begin{array}{r} 87 \\ -26 \\ \hline \end{array}$$
$$\begin{array}{r} 48 \\ -33 \\ \hline \end{array}$$

**B.**
$$\begin{array}{r} 39 \\ -13 \\ \hline \end{array}$$
$$\begin{array}{r} 66 \\ -46 \\ \hline \end{array}$$
$$\begin{array}{r} 38 \\ -14 \\ \hline \end{array}$$
$$\begin{array}{r} 75 \\ -52 \\ \hline \end{array}$$
$$\begin{array}{r} 88 \\ -37 \\ \hline \end{array}$$
$$\begin{array}{r} 74 \\ -24 \\ \hline \end{array}$$

**C.**
$$\begin{array}{r} 47 \\ -15 \\ \hline \end{array}$$
$$\begin{array}{r} 96 \\ -73 \\ \hline \end{array}$$
$$\begin{array}{r} 58 \\ -54 \\ \hline \end{array}$$
$$\begin{array}{r} 81 \\ -21 \\ \hline \end{array}$$
$$\begin{array}{r} 57 \\ -33 \\ \hline \end{array}$$
$$\begin{array}{r} 49 \\ -25 \\ \hline \end{array}$$

**D.**
$$\begin{array}{r} 36 \\ -14 \\ \hline \end{array}$$
$$\begin{array}{r} 87 \\ -77 \\ \hline \end{array}$$
$$\begin{array}{r} 70 \\ -30 \\ \hline \end{array}$$
$$\begin{array}{r} 65 \\ -50 \\ \hline \end{array}$$
$$\begin{array}{r} 99 \\ -73 \\ \hline \end{array}$$
$$\begin{array}{r} 28 \\ -12 \\ \hline \end{array}$$

**E.**
$$\begin{array}{r} 97 \\ -25 \\ \hline \end{array}$$
$$\begin{array}{r} 64 \\ -23 \\ \hline \end{array}$$
$$\begin{array}{r} 72 \\ -22 \\ \hline \end{array}$$
$$\begin{array}{r} 89 \\ -55 \\ \hline \end{array}$$
$$\begin{array}{r} 55 \\ -14 \\ \hline \end{array}$$
$$\begin{array}{r} 83 \\ -20 \\ \hline \end{array}$$

**Summer Bridge Math** RB-904087

# Two-Digit Subtraction with Regrouping

| | | |
|---|---|---|
| 1. Subtract the ones column. You cannot subtract 7 from 2, so regroup. | 2. To regroup, take I ten from the 4 tens, leaving 3 tens. Add the ten to the ones to make 12 ones. Subtract. Twelve minus 7 equals 5. | 3. Subtract the tens column. Three tens minus 2 tens equals I ten. |

$$\begin{array}{r} 4\,\mathbf{2} \\ -\ 2\,\mathbf{7} \\ \hline \end{array}$$

$$\begin{array}{r} \overset{3}{\cancel{4}}{}^{1}2 \\ -\ 2\ 7 \\ \hline \mathbf{5} \end{array}$$

$$\begin{array}{r} \overset{3}{\cancel{4}}{}^{1}2 \\ -\ \mathbf{2}\ 7 \\ \hline \mathbf{1}\ 5 \end{array}$$

## Study the example above. Then, solve each problem.

**A.**

| 36 | 98 | 28 | 41 | 33 | 67 |
|---|---|---|---|---|---|
| − 17 | − 19 | − 9 | − 15 | − 17 | − 18 |

**B.**

| 72 | 85 | 43 | 96 | 64 | 50 |
|---|---|---|---|---|---|
| − 53 | − 27 | − 29 | − 37 | − 36 | − 18 |

**C.**

| 47 | 94 | 75 | 61 | 33 | 82 |
|---|---|---|---|---|---|
| − 19 | − 26 | − 39 | − 22 | − 19 | − 35 |

**D.**

| 71 | 86 | 94 | 65 | 92 | 53 |
|---|---|---|---|---|---|
| − 46 | − 47 | − 35 | − 27 | − 44 | − 29 |

**E.**

| 76 | 64 | 76 | 52 | 83 | 68 |
|---|---|---|---|---|---|
| − 38 | − 35 | − 27 | − 44 | − 25 | − 49 |

# Three-Digit Subtraction

| 1. Subtract the ones column. | 2. Subtract the tens column. | 3. Subtract the hundreds column. |
|---|---|---|
| 5 6 **4**<br>− 1 3 **2**<br>**2** | 5 **6** 4<br>− 1 **3** 2<br>**3** 2 | **5** 6 4<br>− **1** 3 2<br>**4** 3 2 |

**Study the example above. Then, solve each problem.**

**A.**
$$684 - 253 \qquad 634 - 421 \qquad 835 - 610 \qquad 738 - 502 \qquad 325 - 102$$

**B.**
$$874 - 321 \qquad 647 - 325 \qquad 958 - 146 \qquad 363 - 242 \qquad 567 - 362$$

**C.**
$$283 - 220 \qquad 488 - 351 \qquad 695 - 233 \qquad 719 - 305 \qquad 894 - 752$$

**D.**
$$975 - 342 \qquad 767 - 425 \qquad 836 - 132 \qquad 547 - 235 \qquad 658 - 510$$

**E.**
$$393 - 173 \qquad 649 - 235 \qquad 786 - 526 \qquad 999 - 683 \qquad 887 - 346$$

**Summer Bridge Math** RB-904087

© Rainbow Bridge Publishing

# Three-Digit Subtraction with Regrouping

1. Subtract the ones column. You cannot subtract 6 from 4, so regroup. Take 1 ten from the 3 tens. Add the ten to the ones to make 14 ones. Subtract.

$$
\begin{array}{r}
5 \overset{2}{\cancel{3}} \overset{1}{4} \\
- 2\ 5\ 6 \\
\hline
8
\end{array}
$$

2. Look at the tens column. You cannot subtract 5 tens from 2 tens, so regroup. Take 1 hundred from the 5 hundreds. Add the hundred to the tens to make 12 tens. Subtract.

$$
\begin{array}{r}
\overset{4}{\cancel{5}} \overset{12}{\cancel{3}} \overset{1}{4} \\
- 2\ 5\ 6 \\
\hline
7\ 8
\end{array}
$$

3. Subtract the hundreds column.

$$
\begin{array}{r}
\overset{4}{\cancel{5}} \overset{12}{\cancel{3}} \overset{1}{4} \\
- 2\ 5\ 6 \\
\hline
2\ 7\ 8
\end{array}
$$

## Study the example above. Then, solve each problem.

**A.**
|   |   |   |   |   |
|---|---|---|---|---|
| 837 | 516 | 825 | 713 | 624 |
| − 138 | − 247 | − 356 | − 284 | − 367 |

**B.**
|   |   |   |   |   |
|---|---|---|---|---|
| 283 | 567 | 928 | 785 | 497 |
| − 96 | − 275 | − 189 | − 496 | − 269 |

**C.**
|   |   |   |   |   |
|---|---|---|---|---|
| 553 | 476 | 764 | 676 | 952 |
| − 129 | − 138 | − 335 | − 227 | − 344 |

**D.**
|   |   |   |   |   |
|---|---|---|---|---|
| 837 | 689 | 941 | 277 | 765 |
| − 253 | − 496 | − 250 | − 193 | − 295 |

**Summer Bridge Math** RB-904087

# Four-Digit Subtraction

## Study the examples on pages 26–29. Then, solve each problem.

**A.**

| 9,375 | 2,772 | 3,943 | 5,814 | 5,932 |
|---|---|---|---|---|
| − 4,969 | − 1,476 | − 1,876 | − 2,867 | − 3,845 |

**B.**

| 7,403 | 9,800 | 5,639 | 7,860 | 6,657 |
|---|---|---|---|---|
| − 2,675 | − 3,765 | − 1,879 | − 1,895 | − 5,575 |

**C.**

| 8,207 | 9,730 | 7,796 | 3,905 | 5,667 |
|---|---|---|---|---|
| − 4,648 | − 4,698 | − 2,994 | − 1,847 | − 2,909 |

**D.**

| 8,436 | 6,943 | 3,845 | 8,560 | 9,454 |
|---|---|---|---|---|
| − 7,527 | − 2,880 | − 1,966 | − 2,483 | − 2,087 |

**E.**

| 7,571 | 5,965 | 4,739 | 7,430 | 8,956 |
|---|---|---|---|---|
| − 3,875 | − 1,879 | − 3,465 | − 2,767 | − 3,979 |

**Summer Bridge Math** RB-904087

# Subtraction with Regrouping Practice

**Study the examples on pages 26–29. Then, solve each problem.**

**A.**
| 3,621 | 4,197 | 2,479 | 5,076 |
|---|---|---|---|
| − 1,283 | − 468 | − 890 | − 1,256 |

**B.**
| 9,616 | 3,804 | 8,941 | 982 |
|---|---|---|---|
| − 758 | − 1,192 | − 173 | − 497 |

**C.**
| 8,263 | 7,603 | 9,550 | 645 |
|---|---|---|---|
| − 4,458 | − 215 | − 4,229 | − 187 |

**D.**
| 850 | 2,972 |
|---|---|
| − 76 | − 493 |

Write your own subtraction problem that uses regrouping two times.

**Summer Bridge Math** RB-904087

# Two-Digit Mixed Practice

**Study the examples on pages 19–20 and 26–27. Then, solve each problem.**

**A.**

$$87 - 29$$  $$29 + 37$$  $$51 - 23$$  $$26 + 45$$  $$35 + 57$$

**B.**

$$91 - 67$$  $$86 - 27$$  $$71 - 52$$  $$62 + 19$$  $$53 - 21$$

**C.**

$$47 + 13$$  $$84 + 58$$  $$31 - 19$$  $$93 - 36$$  $$44 + 48$$

**D.**

$$72 - 39$$  $$28 + 57$$  $$49 - 31$$  $$62 + 25$$  $$98 - 37$$

**E.**

$$88 - 49$$  $$29 + 18$$  $$77 - 58$$  $$66 + 26$$  $$11 + 78$$

**F.**

$$87 + 26$$  $$27 + 47$$  $$53 - 34$$  $$27 + 55$$  $$34 - 18$$

**Summer Bridge Math** RB-904087

© Rainbow Bridge Publishing

# Three-Digit Mixed Practice

**Study the examples on pages 21–22 and 28–29. Then, solve each problem.**

**A.**

$$187 + 838$$

$$492 - 185$$

$$886 + 340$$

$$725 + 287$$

$$630 - 168$$

**B.**

$$317 + 415$$

$$617 + 304$$

$$227 - 109$$

$$380 + 739$$

$$817 - 468$$

**C.**

$$374 - 176$$

$$537 + 285$$

$$620 - 182$$

$$972 + 409$$

$$732 - 269$$

**D.**

$$236 + 587$$

$$279 + 373$$

$$660 - 153$$

$$456 + 464$$

$$770 - 262$$

**E.**

$$803 - 377$$

$$917 - 458$$

$$746 + 336$$

$$548 + 476$$

$$476 + 389$$

**F.**

$$847 + 387$$

$$689 - 295$$

$$550 + 281$$

$$627 + 277$$

$$649 + 279$$

**Summer Bridge Math** RB-904087

# Out of This World!

**Start from the center numeral and work out to solve each problem.**

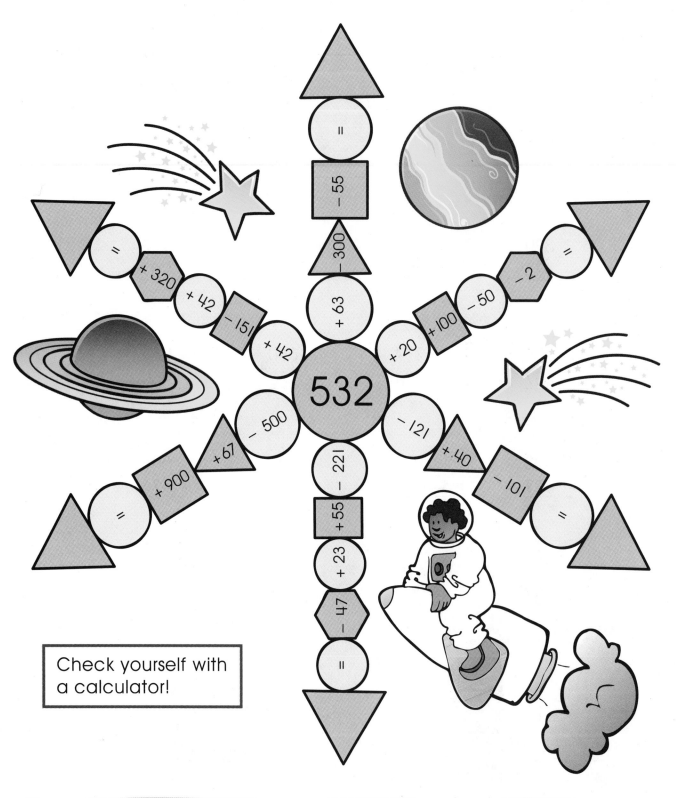

Check yourself with a calculator!

# Introduction to Multiplication

To **multiply** means to use repeated addition. The answer to a multiplication problem is called the **product**. The numbers being multiplied are called **factors**. To more easily understand, imagine making equal groups. Then, add all of the groups together. Multiplication looks like this:

4 + 4 + 4

3 groups of 4

3 x 4 ← factors

12 ← product

**Study the example above. Then, write an addition and multiplication problem for each picture. Find the sum and the product.**

**A.**

XXXXX
XXXXX
XXXXX

☐ + ☐ + ☐ = ☐

☐ x ☐ = ☐

**B.**

☆ ☆ ☆
☆ ☆ ☆

☐ + ☐ = ☐

☐ x ☐ = ☐

**C.**

☐ + ☐ + ☐ + ☐ = ☐

☐ x ☐ = ☐

**D.**

@ @ @ @
@ @ @ @

☐ + ☐ = ☐

☐ x ☐ = ☐

**E.**

X X X
X X X
X X X

☐ + ☐ + ☐ = ☐

☐ x ☐ = ☐

**F.**

☐ + ☐ + ☐ = ☐

☐ x ☐ = ☐

**G.**

☐ + ☐ + ☐ = ☐

☐ x ☐ = ☐

**H.**

@ @ @ @ @
@ @ @ @ @

☐ + ☐ = ☐

☐ x ☐ = ☐

 **Summer Bridge Math** RB-904087

# Multiplication Chart

**Complete the chart. Then, answer the questions.**

| x | 1 | 2 | 3 | 4 | 5 | 6 | 7 | 8 | 9 |
|---|---|---|---|---|---|---|---|---|---|
| 1 | 1 |   |   |   |   |   |   |   |   |
| 2 |   |   |   |   |   |   |   |   |   |
| 3 |   |   |   |   |   |   |   |   |   |
| 4 |   |   |   |   |   |   |   |   |   |
| 5 |   |   |   |   |   |   |   |   |   |
| 6 |   |   |   |   |   |   |   |   |   |
| 7 |   |   |   |   |   |   |   |   |   |
| 8 |   |   |   |   |   |   |   |   |   |
| 9 |   |   |   |   |   |   |   |   |   |

**A.** What does any number times 1 equal? _____

**B.** What pattern do you see in the twos? _____

_____

**C.** What pattern do you see in the fives? _____

_____

**D.** Add the digits for each answer in the nines. What number does each

answer equal? _____

**E.** 3 x 4 = 12. What does 4 x 3 equal? _____

**Summer Bridge Math** RB-904087

# Finding the Facts

Study the example on page 35 or the multiplication chart on page 36. Then, find the product for each pair of factors below. Use the code to find the letters. Write the letters on the lines to answer the two riddles.

| A | B | C | D | E | F | G | H | I | J | K | L | M | N | O | P | Q | R | S | T | U | V | W | X | Y | Z |
|---|---|---|---|---|---|---|---|---|---|---|---|---|---|---|---|---|---|---|---|---|---|---|---|---|---|
| 64 | 4 | 42 | 7 | 24 | 16 | 0 | 18 | 40 | 11 | 19 | 49 | 59 | 25 | 12 | 13 | 21 | 56 | 8 | 54 | 32 | 28 | 45 | 60 | 9 | 14 |

## What can you hold in your left hand but not in your right hand?

___  ___  ___  ___
3 x 3  6 x 2  8 x 4  7 x 8

___  ___  ___  ___  ___
8 x 7  5 x 8  1 x 0  6 x 3  6 x 9

___  ___  ___  ___  ___ !
8 x 3  7 x 7  2 x 2  3 x 4  9 x 5

## Why is it so easy to weigh fish?

___  ___  ___  ___  ___  ___  ___
4 x 1  6 x 4  6 x 7  8 x 8  4 x 8  2 x 4  3 x 8

___  ___  ___  ___      ___  ___  ___
4 x 4  8 x 5  1 x 8  9 x 2    3 x 6  8 x 8  7 x 4  4 x 6

___  ___  ___  ___  ___      ___  ___  ___
9 x 6  2 x 9  8 x 3  5 x 8  7 x 8    3 x 4  9 x 5  5 x 5

___  ___  ___  ___  ___  ___ !
4 x 2  7 x 6  8 x 8  7 x 7  6 x 4  8 x 1

**Summer Bridge Math** RB-904087

# Multiplication Practice

**Study the example on page 35. Then, solve each problem.**

**A.**

| 2 | 3 | 5 | 1 | 6 |
|---|---|---|---|---|
| x 2 | x 2 | x 3 | x 6 | x 2 |

**B.**

| 2 | 5 | 2 | 2 | 2 |
|---|---|---|---|---|
| x 8 | x 2 | x 6 | x 4 | x 1 |

**C.**

| 7 | 3 | 9 | 8 | 4 |
|---|---|---|---|---|
| x 2 | x 6 | x 2 | x 2 | x 5 |

**D.**

| 3 | 6 | 4 | 3 | 8 |
|---|---|---|---|---|
| x 9 | x 5 | x 6 | x 7 | x 3 |

**E.**

| 4 | 5 | 5 | 7 | 8 |
|---|---|---|---|---|
| x 4 | x 6 | x 8 | x 9 | x 8 |

**F.**

| 5 | 8 | 7 | 5 | 4 |
|---|---|---|---|---|
| x 4 | x 9 | x 6 | x 7 | x 8 |

**G.**

| 6 | 7 | 8 | 9 | 9 |
|---|---|---|---|---|
| x 6 | x 4 | x 7 | x 9 | x 4 |

**H.**

| 4 | 5 | 5 | 6 | 4 |
|---|---|---|---|---|
| x 5 | x 5 | x 9 | x 8 | x 7 |

**Summer Bridge Math** RB-904087

# Two-Digit Multiplication

First, multiply the ones. Then, multiply the tens. Add.

$$\begin{array}{r} 1\mathbf{2} \\ \times\ \ \mathbf{3} \\ \hline \mathbf{6} \end{array}\ +\ \begin{array}{r} 1\mathbf{2} \\ \times\ \ \mathbf{3} \\ \hline \mathbf{3\,0} \end{array}\ =\ \mathbf{36}$$

Shortcut:

$$\begin{array}{r} 1\,2 \\ \times\ \ 3 \\ \hline \mathbf{3\,6} \end{array}$$

Multiply the ones.
Multiply the tens.

**Study the example above. Then, solve each problem.**

**A.**

| 12 | 11 | 13 | 13 |
|---|---|---|---|
| x 4 | x 2 | x 2 | x 3 |

**B.**

| 11 | 14 | 12 | 11 |
|---|---|---|---|
| x 3 | x 2 | x 3 | x 4 |

**C.**

| 13 | 11 | 22 | 32 |
|---|---|---|---|
| x 1 | x 6 | x 3 | x 2 |

**D.**

| 42 | 24 | 22 | 21 |
|---|---|---|---|
| x 2 | x 2 | x 2 | x 3 |

**E.**

| 33 | 32 | 31 | 31 |
|---|---|---|---|
| x 3 | x 3 | x 3 | x 2 |

# Two-Digit Multiplication with Regrouping

First, multiply the ones. Then, multiply the tens. Add.

$$\begin{array}{r} 1\ 3 \\ \times\ 6 \\ \hline 1\ 8 \end{array} + \begin{array}{r} 1\ 3 \\ \times\ 6 \\ \hline 6\ 0 \end{array} = 78$$

Shortcut:
Multiply the ones.
Regroup the tens.

$$\begin{array}{r} 1\phantom{0} \\ 1\ 3 \\ \times\ 6 \\ \hline 7\ 8 \end{array}$$

Multiply the tens.
6 x 10 = 60
Add the extra ten.
60 + 10 = 70

## Study the example above. Then, solve each problem.

**A.**

| 15 | 14 | 13 | 24 | 22 |
|---|---|---|---|---|
| x 6 | x 5 | x 7 | x 3 | x 5 |

**B.**

| 12 | 25 | 32 | 23 | 14 |
|---|---|---|---|---|
| x 7 | x 4 | x 6 | x 7 | x 8 |

**C.**

| 26 | 52 | 44 | 34 | 13 |
|---|---|---|---|---|
| x 3 | x 6 | x 5 | x 6 | x 9 |

**D.**

| 84 | 45 | 32 | 16 | 28 |
|---|---|---|---|---|
| x 3 | x 6 | x 9 | x 7 | x 2 |

**E.**

| 35 | 18 | 22 | 34 | 47 |
|---|---|---|---|---|
| x 6 | x 7 | x 7 | x 5 | x 3 |

**F.**

| 19 | 33 | 42 | 63 | 83 |
|---|---|---|---|---|
| x 2 | x 6 | x 8 | x 4 | x 5 |

**Summer Bridge Math** RB-904087

# Three-Digit Multiplication

## Study the examples on pages 39 and 40. Then, solve each problem.

**A.**

| 311 | 248 | 225 | 283 | 999 | 274 |
|-----|-----|-----|-----|-----|-----|
| x 8 | x 2 | x 4 | x 3 | x 2 | x 2 |

**B.**

| 143 | 215 | 103 | 150 | 103 | 208 |
|-----|-----|-----|-----|-----|-----|
| x 7 | x 3 | x 8 | x 5 | x 9 | x 4 |

**C.**

| 401 | 210 | 252 | 200 | 111 | 521 |
|-----|-----|-----|-----|-----|-----|
| x 9 | x 4 | x 3 | x 6 | x 8 | x 7 |

**D.**

| 411 | 517 | 108 | 162 | 136 | 510 |
|-----|-----|-----|-----|-----|-----|
| x 9 | x 6 | x 8 | x 4 | x 3 | x 7 |

**E.**

| 907 | 485 | 271 | 704 | 112 | 235 |
|-----|-----|-----|-----|-----|-----|
| x 7 | x 2 | x 9 | x 8 | x 6 | x 5 |

**F.**

| 362 | 125 | 422 | 891 | 107 | 790 |
|-----|-----|-----|-----|-----|-----|
| x 3 | x 8 | x 4 | x 6 | x 9 | x 5 |

# Multiplying Money

When multiplying money, be sure to include the dollar sign and the decimal in your answer.

$$\begin{array}{r} {}^{5}\ {}^{2} \\ \$5.63 \\ \times \quad 8 \\ \hline \$45.04 \end{array} \qquad \begin{array}{r} {}^{5}\ {}^{1} \\ \$1.93 \\ \times \quad 6 \\ \hline \$11.58 \end{array}$$

**Study the example above. Then, find the products. Be sure to include the money symbols.**

**A.**

$$\begin{array}{r} \$7.30 \\ \times \quad 5 \\ \hline \end{array} \qquad \begin{array}{r} \$3.41 \\ \times \quad 8 \\ \hline \end{array} \qquad \begin{array}{r} \$8.24 \\ \times \quad 3 \\ \hline \end{array} \qquad \begin{array}{r} \$6.15 \\ \times \quad 7 \\ \hline \end{array}$$

**B.**

$$\begin{array}{r} \$0.68 \\ \times \quad 2 \\ \hline \end{array} \qquad \begin{array}{r} \$1.98 \\ \times \quad 4 \\ \hline \end{array} \qquad \begin{array}{r} \$3.62 \\ \times \quad 6 \\ \hline \end{array} \qquad \begin{array}{r} \$2.99 \\ \times \quad 5 \\ \hline \end{array}$$

**C.**

$$\begin{array}{r} \$1.37 \\ \times \quad 7 \\ \hline \end{array} \qquad \begin{array}{r} \$0.91 \\ \times \quad 9 \\ \hline \end{array} \qquad \begin{array}{r} \$4.00 \\ \times \quad 8 \\ \hline \end{array} \qquad \begin{array}{r} \$1.23 \\ \times \quad 9 \\ \hline \end{array}$$

**D.**

$$\begin{array}{r} \$0.11 \\ \times \quad 8 \\ \hline \end{array} \qquad \begin{array}{r} \$3.82 \\ \times \quad 3 \\ \hline \end{array} \qquad \begin{array}{r} \$0.74 \\ \times \quad 4 \\ \hline \end{array} \qquad \begin{array}{r} \$6.80 \\ \times \quad 7 \\ \hline \end{array}$$

**Summer Bridge Math** RB-904087

# Introduction to Division

To **divide** means to make equal groups or to share equally. The answer to a division problem is called the **quotient**. Division looks like this:

Total    # of    # in
    in    groups   each
              group

$12 \div 3 = 4$

Total    # of    # in
         groups   each
               group

$10 \div 2 = 5$

**Study the examples above. Then, circle equal groups to find the quotient for each picture.**

**A.**

$10 \div 5 = \boxed{\phantom{0}}$

**B.**

$15 \div 3 = \boxed{\phantom{0}}$

**C.**

$6 \div 3 = \boxed{\phantom{0}}$

**D.**

$8 \div 2 = \boxed{\phantom{0}}$

**E.**

$9 \div 3 = \boxed{\phantom{0}}$

**F.**

$12 \div 4 = \boxed{\phantom{0}}$

**G.**

$12 \div 6 = \boxed{\phantom{0}}$

**H.**

$18 \div 3 = \boxed{\phantom{0}}$

**I.**

$14 \div 7 = \boxed{\phantom{0}}$

**43**

# Understanding Division

Twenty total objects are put into 4 groups. There are 5 objects in each group.

$$20 \div 4 = 5$$

20 divided into 4 groups

$$4\overline{)20}^{\,5}$$

**Study the examples above and on page 43. Then, solve each problem. Draw a picture. Write the equation.**

**A.** 21 divided into 3 groups

_____

**B.** 30 divided into 5 groups

_____

**C.** 36 divided into 9 groups

_____

**D.** 18 divided into 6 groups

_____

**Summer Bridge Math** RB-904087

# Using Division Signs

We read this problem as "12 **divided** by 3 **equals** 4." Twelve put into 3 equal groups equals 4 in each group.

$12 \div 3 = \underline{\phantom{4}}4\phantom{4}$

$$3\overline{)12}^{\,4}$$

**Study the examples above and on pages 43 and 44. Then, solve each problem. Draw a picture.**

**A.**  $9 \div 3 = \underline{\phantom{xxxx}}$

  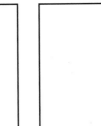

**B.**  $8 \div 2 = \underline{\phantom{xxxx}}$

**C.**  $6 \div 2 = \underline{\phantom{xxxx}}$

**D.**  $16 \div 4 = \underline{\phantom{xxxx}}$

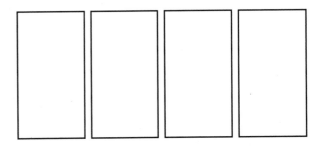

**E.**  $12 \div 6 = \underline{\phantom{xxxx}}$

**F.**  $18 \div 3 = \underline{\phantom{xxxx}}$

**Summer Bridge Math** RB-904087

# Dividing by a Single-Digit Numeral

Knowing your multiplication facts makes these division problems a snap!

**Study the examples on pages 43–45. Then, solve each problem. Refer to the multiplication chart on page 36 if you need help.**

**A.**  $6\overline{)36}$     $7\overline{)42}$     $8\overline{)56}$     $5\overline{)45}$

**B.**  $3\overline{)21}$     $9\overline{)63}$     $4\overline{)36}$     $6\overline{)54}$

**C.**  $5\overline{)35}$     $3\overline{)27}$     $2\overline{)18}$     $7\overline{)49}$

**D.**  $3\overline{)18}$     $6\overline{)24}$     $4\overline{)32}$     $9\overline{)54}$

**E.**  $4\overline{)16}$     $2\overline{)14}$     $5\overline{)25}$     $8\overline{)64}$

**F.**  $9\overline{)36}$     $4\overline{)24}$     $7\overline{)35}$     $5\overline{)30}$

**G.**  $6\overline{)42}$     $2\overline{)16}$     $6\overline{)24}$     $5\overline{)40}$

**H.**  $3\overline{)24}$     $7\overline{)21}$     $8\overline{)72}$     $9\overline{)81}$

**Summer Bridge Math** RB-904087

# Division with Remainders

Divisor → $3\overline{)19}$ ← Dividend

1. Think. How many times will 3 go into 19? 3 x 6 = 18.
2. Then, subtract. What is left is the **remainder**.

$$\begin{array}{r} 6\ r1 \\ 3\overline{)19} \\ -18 \\ \hline 1 \end{array}$$

**Study the example above. Then, solve each problem.**

**A.** $2\overline{)15}$ $\qquad$ $3\overline{)17}$ $\qquad$ $4\overline{)19}$ $\qquad$ $6\overline{)22}$

**B.** $4\overline{)25}$ $\qquad$ $5\overline{)18}$ $\qquad$ $7\overline{)23}$ $\qquad$ $8\overline{)43}$

**C.** $9\overline{)70}$ $\qquad$ $2\overline{)19}$ $\qquad$ $4\overline{)21}$ $\qquad$ $5\overline{)24}$

**D.** $7\overline{)30}$ $\qquad$ $6\overline{)13}$ $\qquad$ $8\overline{)25}$ $\qquad$ $5\overline{)32}$

**E.** $4\overline{)17}$ $\qquad$ $7\overline{)25}$ $\qquad$ $9\overline{)42}$ $\qquad$ $8\overline{)38}$

**F.** $5\overline{)19}$ $\qquad$ $7\overline{)18}$ $\qquad$ $8\overline{)17}$ $\qquad$ $6\overline{)32}$

# Division Practice

**Study the examples on pages 43–45 and 47. Then, solve each problem.**

**A.**   $3\overline{)9}$    $4\overline{)12}$    $5\overline{)15}$    $7\overline{)28}$    $8\overline{)32}$

**B.**   $9\overline{)72}$    $5\overline{)35}$    $6\overline{)42}$    $8\overline{)64}$    $7\overline{)49}$

**C.**   $3\overline{)19}$    $4\overline{)15}$    $5\overline{)18}$    $7\overline{)22}$    $9\overline{)29}$

**D.**   $6\overline{)37}$    $7\overline{)39}$    $8\overline{)25}$    $5\overline{)27}$    $4\overline{)34}$

**E.**   $5\overline{)45}$    $2\overline{)12}$    $3\overline{)24}$    $6\overline{)36}$    $4\overline{)24}$

**F.**   $7\overline{)50}$    $8\overline{)92}$    $6\overline{)20}$    $5\overline{)48}$    $3\overline{)16}$

Multiplication depends on equal groups. You can use multiplication basic facts to help you divide. The two are related, like families. They are called **fact families**. It looks like this:

4 groups of 3
$4 \times 3 = 12$

12 divided into 4 equal groups
$12 \div 4 = 3$

**Study the example above. Then, use the missing factor to help you find the quotient.**

**A.**
$2 \times \boxed{\phantom{0}} = 8$

$8 \div 2 = \boxed{\phantom{0}}$

**B.**
$3 \times \boxed{\phantom{0}} = 9$

$9 \div 3 = \boxed{\phantom{0}}$

**C.**
$4 \times \boxed{\phantom{0}} = 16$

$16 \div 4 = \boxed{\phantom{0}}$

**D.**
$8 \times \boxed{\phantom{0}} = 40$

$40 \div 8 = \boxed{\phantom{0}}$

**E.**
$5 \times \boxed{\phantom{0}} = 25$

$25 \div 5 = \boxed{\phantom{0}}$

**F.**
$6 \times \boxed{\phantom{0}} = 18$

$18 \div 6 = \boxed{\phantom{0}}$

**G.**
$4 \times \boxed{\phantom{0}} = 12$

$12 \div 4 = \boxed{\phantom{0}}$

**H.**
$7 \times \boxed{\phantom{0}} = 42$

$42 \div 7 = \boxed{\phantom{0}}$

**I.**
$3 \times \boxed{\phantom{0}} = 15$

$15 \div 3 = \boxed{\phantom{0}}$

**J.**
$9 \times \boxed{\phantom{0}} = 81$

$81 \div 9 = \boxed{\phantom{0}}$

**K.**
$2 \times \boxed{\phantom{0}} = 10$

$10 \div 2 = \boxed{\phantom{0}}$

**L.**
$2 \times \boxed{\phantom{0}} = 4$

$4 \div 2 = \boxed{\phantom{0}}$

**M.**
$5 \times \boxed{\phantom{0}} = 20$

$20 \div 5 = \boxed{\phantom{0}}$

**N.**
$3 \times \boxed{\phantom{0}} = 6$

$6 \div 3 = \boxed{\phantom{0}}$

**O.**
$6 \times \boxed{\phantom{0}} = 36$

$36 \div 6 = \boxed{\phantom{0}}$

# Fact Families

A **fact family** is made up of three numbers that are related. The numbers can be used in a set of math problems. Just like addition and subtraction facts, multiplication and division facts are related.

$$\underline{\phantom{2}2\phantom{2}} \times \underline{\phantom{2}3\phantom{2}} = \underline{\phantom{2}6\phantom{2}}$$
$$\underline{\phantom{2}3\phantom{2}} \times \underline{\phantom{2}2\phantom{2}} = \underline{\phantom{2}6\phantom{2}}$$
$$\underline{\phantom{2}6\phantom{2}} \div \underline{\phantom{2}3\phantom{2}} = \underline{\phantom{2}2\phantom{2}}$$
$$\underline{\phantom{2}6\phantom{2}} \div \underline{\phantom{2}2\phantom{2}} = \underline{\phantom{2}3\phantom{2}}$$

**Study the example above. Then, write 2 multiplication and 2 division equations for each fact family.**

**A.**

_____ X _____ = _____

_____ X _____ = _____

_____ ÷ _____ = _____

_____ ÷ _____ = _____

**B.**

_____ X _____ = _____

_____ X _____ = _____

_____ ÷ _____ = _____

_____ ÷ _____ = _____

**C.**

_____ X _____ = _____

_____ X _____ = _____

_____ ÷ _____ = _____

_____ ÷ _____ = _____

**D.**

_____ X _____ = _____

_____ X _____ = _____

_____ ÷ _____ = _____

_____ ÷ _____ = _____

**Summer Bridge Math** RB-904087

# Mixed Practice

**Study the examples on pages 35 and 43–45. Then, solve each problem.**

**A.**
$$6 \times 8 \qquad 7 \times 3 \qquad 8 \times 2 \qquad 9 \times 4 \qquad 2 \times 7$$

**B.**
$$4 \times 9 \qquad 3 \times 8 \qquad 4 \times 4 \qquad 6 \times 2 \qquad 3 \times 5$$

**C.**
$$8 \times 8 \qquad 6 \times 5 \qquad 2 \times 3 \qquad 4 \times 7 \qquad 2 \times 9$$

**D.**
$$5 \times 6 \qquad 8 \times 7 \qquad 4 \times 5 \qquad 7 \times 7 \qquad 9 \times 8$$

**E.**
$$9\overline{)81} \qquad 7\overline{)35} \qquad 4\overline{)32} \qquad 6\overline{)48}$$

**F.**
$$5\overline{)45} \qquad 4\overline{)24} \qquad 9\overline{)63} \qquad 8\overline{)56}$$

**G.**
$$9\overline{)72} \qquad 7\overline{)42} \qquad 6\overline{)18} \qquad 3\overline{)21}$$

**H.**
$$8\overline{)40} \qquad 6\overline{)54} \qquad 8\overline{)64} \qquad 9\overline{)36}$$

The short hand is called the **hour hand**. It tells the hour. The long hand is the **minute hand**. It tells the minutes. On the left, the clock's hour hand is on the 8. The minute hand is on the 12. It shows 8 o'clock. On the right, the clock's minute hand is on the 6. It shows 8:30. We say this as "eight-thirty."

8:00

8:30

**Study the examples above. Then, write the time shown on each clock.**

**A.**

_____ : _____

_____ : _____

_____ : _____

**B.**

_____ : _____

_____ : _____

_____ : _____

# Five-Minute Intervals

The minute hand takes 5 minutes to move from one number on the clock to the next. We count by fives as the minute hand moves to the next number. To read this clock, we say:

20 minutes past 3:00

3:20

40 minutes past 9:00

9:40

**Study the examples above. Then, write each time two ways.**

**A.** ☐ minutes past ☐ : ☐

☐ : ☐

**B.** ☐ minutes past ☐ : ☐

☐ : ☐

**C.** ☐ minutes past ☐ : ☐

☐ : ☐

**D.** ☐ minutes past ☐ : ☐

☐ : ☐

**E.** ☐ minutes past ☐ : ☐

☐ : ☐

**F.** ☐ minutes past ☐ : ☐

☐ : ☐

**G.** ☐ minutes past ☐ : ☐

☐ : ☐

**H.** ☐ minutes past ☐ : ☐

☐ : ☐

**I.** ☐ minutes past ☐ : ☐

☐ : ☐

**J.** ☐ minutes past ☐ : ☐

☐ : ☐

**53**

# Drawing Hands on Clocks

**Study the examples on pages 52 and 53. Then, draw the hands on each clock to show the time.**

**A.**

8:35

**B.**

9:50

**C.**

6:47

**D.**

12:23

**E.**

10:25

**F.**

7:53

**G.**

11:08

**H.**

4:47

**I.**

6:17

# Introduction to Money

These are five commonly used coins in the United States.

50¢    25¢    10¢    5¢    1¢

The amount that coins are worth is called their **value**. You can find the total value of coins by adding one amount to another amount. This is called **counting on**.

50¢ → 75¢ → 85¢ → 90¢ → 95¢ → 96¢ → 97¢

## Study the example above. Then, count on to find the total value.

**A.**

= ⬜ ¢

**B.**

= ⬜ ¢

**C.**

= ⬜ ¢

**D.**

= ⬜ ¢

**E.**

= ⬜ ¢

**F.**

= ⬜ ¢

**G.**

= ⬜ ¢

**H.**

= ⬜ ¢

**55**

# Skip Counting Coins

It is easier to count coins if you **skip count** by the coin's value.

<u>10</u> ¢ <u>20</u> ¢ <u>30</u> ¢ <u>35</u> ¢ <u>40</u> ¢ <u>45</u> ¢ <u>50</u> ¢ <u>55</u> ¢   Total <u>55</u> ¢

**Study the example above and the coin values on page 55. Then, practice skip counting using the coins shown.**

**A.**

____¢ ____¢ ____¢ ____¢ ____¢ ____¢ ____¢ ____¢   Total ____¢

**B.**

____¢ ____¢ ____¢ ____¢ ____¢ ____¢ ____¢ ____¢   Total ____¢

**C.**

____¢ ____¢ ____¢ ____¢ ____¢ ____¢ ____¢ ____¢   Total ____¢

**D.**

____¢ ____¢ ____¢ ____¢ ____¢ ____¢ ____¢ ____¢   Total ____¢

**E.**

____¢ ____¢ ____¢ ____¢ ____¢ ____¢ ____¢ ____¢   Total ____¢

**F.**

____¢ ____¢ ____¢ ____¢ ____¢ ____¢ ____¢ ____¢   Total ____¢

We write one dollar as $1.00.
We say $1.35 as "one dollar
and thirty-five cents."

$1.35

$1.00 = 100¢          $5.00          $10.00          $20.00

**Study the money values above and on page 55. Then, count the money to find the total value.**

**A.**

_____

**B.**

_____

**C.**

_____

**D.**

_____

**E.**

_____

**F.**

_____

**Summer Bridge Math** RB-904087

# Calculating Change

> Sometimes when you pay for something, you get **change** back.
> You can figure your change using these steps:
> 1. Begin with the amount you paid the cashier.
> 2. Subtract the amount you owe from the amount you paid. Make sure to keep the **decimal points** lined up.
> 3. The difference is your change.
>
> $$\begin{array}{r} {\scriptstyle 4\ \ 9\ 10} \\ \$\cancel{5}.\cancel{0}\cancel{0} \\ -\ \ 0.75 \\ \hline \$4.25 \end{array}$$
>
> Line up the decimal points. ↑

**Study the example above. Then, find the amount of change that will be given to the customer.**

**A.** Paid    $6.00
    Owe    − 2.10
           $3.90

**B.** Paid    $20.00
    Owe    − 16.20

**C.** Paid    $8.00
    Owe    − 3.95

**D.** Paid    $10.00
    Owe    − 4.60

**E.** Paid    $9.00
    Owe    − 8.50

**F.** Paid    $5.00
    Owe    − .95

**G.** Paid    $16.00
    Owe    − 15.15

**H.** Paid    $20.00
    Owe    − 5.00

**I.** Paid    $2.00
    Owe    − 1.19

**J.** Paid    $4.00
    Owe    − 3.95

**K.** Paid    $10.00
    Owe    − 7.49

**L.** Paid    $12.00
    Owe    − 11.23

**58**

# Standard Measurement

| | | |
|---|---|---|
| inches | = 1 inch | |
| | 1 foot equals 12 inches. | |

**Complete each sentence. Choose the measurement that makes the most sense.**

**A.** My Dad is _____ tall.      6 inches     6 feet

**B.** My math book is _____ wide.     9 inches     9 feet

**C.** My big toe is _____ long.     1 inch

**D.** My new baby sister is _____ long.     20 inches

**Measure the shape at the right with a ruler.**

**E.** What is the length of the rectangle? _____ inches

**F.** What is the width of the rectangle? _____ inches

**G.** Add the measurements of the 4 sides of the rectangle to find its perimeter.

____ inches + ____ inches + ____ inch + ____ inch = _____ inches

# Comparing Linear Measurements

What would you use to measure the distance around your house? What would you use to find the distance to a nearby city? You would probably not use the same unit of measurement for both of these jobs. Compare the common units of measurement listed below.

| Unit | To estimate, use: | Equal to: |
|---|---|---|
| centimeter (cm) | width of your finger | |
| meter (m) | width of a doorway | 100 cm |
| kilometer (km) | distance you walk in 15 minutes | 1000 m |
| inch (in.) | width of two fingers | |
| foot (ft.) | height of this paper | 12 in. |
| yard (yd.) | length of a baseball bat | 3 ft. or 36 in. |
| mile | distance you walk in 25 minutes | 1,760 yd. |

## Use the table above to find the equal measurements.

**A.** 1000 m = _____ km  2 ft. = _____ in.  48 in. = _____ ft.

**B.** 1 ft. = _____ in.  3 ft. = _____ yd.  2 yd. = _____ ft.

**C.** 1 yd. = _____ in.  24 in. = _____ ft.  2000 m = _____ km

**D.** 2 m = _____ cm  4 km = _____ m  36 in. = _____ ft.

## Compare using <, >, or =.

**E.** 1 ft. ◯ 1 yd.  1 ft. ◯ 1 in.

**F.** 4 yd. ◯ 1 mile  1 yd. ◯ 2 ft.

**G.** 4 in. ◯ 4 cm  24 in. ◯ 2 ft.

**H.** 1 ft. ◯ 12 in.  1 mile ◯ 1 km

**60**

# Increments and Weight

Have you ever noticed all of the small lines along the top of a scale? They divide the scale into equal **increments**, or parts. Sometimes, the measurement you want is between two numbers. These measurements are marked with smaller lines. You must find the increment pattern of the smaller lines.

Count by ones.
Scale shows 44.

Count by twos.
Scale shows 36.

Count by fives.
Scale shows 45.

**Study the examples above. Then, read each scale. Circle the best unit of measurement by using the weight chart below.**

| I ounce | I pound | I gram | I kilogram |
|---------|---------|--------|------------|

pounds
ounces

grams
pounds

kilograms
ounces

grams
pounds

pounds
ounces

grams
pounds

**Summer Bridge Math** RB-904087

# Capacity and Temperature

**Capacity** is the amount that a container can hold. Standard capacity can be measured in:

 1 cup (c.)

 1 pint (pt.) 2 c.

 1 quart (qt.) 2 pt. 4 c.

1 gallon (gal.) 4 qt. 8 pt. 16 c.

**Study the measurements above. Then, compare using <, >, or =.**

**A.** 2 c. ◯ 2 gal.    2 pt. ◯ 1 qt.    5 c. ◯ 1 qt.

**B.** 3 pt. ◯ 2 qt.    3 qt. ◯ 1 gal.    1 gal. ◯ 17 c.

**C.** 1 gal. ◯ 4 qt.    3 c. ◯ 1 pt.    2 qt. ◯ 4 pt.

Temperatures can be measured using either side of a thermometer. One side shows **Fahrenheit (°F)**, which is the standard unit of measure. The other side shows **Celsius (°C)**, which is the metric unit of measure. If the reading is below zero, write the temperature using a minus sign.
**Example:** −23°F

68°F 20°C room temperature Comfy!

212°F 100°C Water boils.

Whew! Give me a fan, quick! 95°F 35°C

32°F 0°C Water freezes.

**Write the temperature in °F and °C for each thermometer. Then, list two articles of clothing you would wear that day.**

**D.** _____°F _____°C

I would wear _____

**E.** _____°F _____°C

I would wear _____

A **fraction** tells about equal parts of a whole. The top number is the **numerator**. It tells how many parts are shaded. The bottom number is the **denominator**. It tells how many parts in all.

Parts shaded ➡️ $\dfrac{1}{6}$

Parts in all ➡️

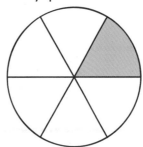

## Study the example above. Then, write each fraction.

**A.**

**B.**

**C.**

**D.**

**E.**

**F.**

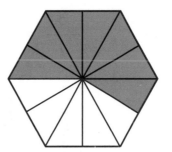

**Summer Bridge Math** RB-904087

# Equivalent Fractions

**Equivalent fractions** are fractions that are equal. To find equivalent fractions, multiply the numerator and the denominator of a fraction by the same number.

$$\frac{1 \times (2)}{2 \times (2)} = \frac{2}{4} \qquad \frac{1 \times (3)}{2 \times (3)} = \frac{3}{6}$$

**Study the example above. Then, fill in the missing numerals to show equivalent fractions.**

**A.** $\dfrac{1}{3} = \dfrac{\square}{6} = \dfrac{\square}{9} = \dfrac{4}{\square} = \dfrac{5}{\square}$

**B.** $\dfrac{1}{4} = \dfrac{\square}{8} = \dfrac{\square}{12} = \dfrac{4}{\square} = \dfrac{\square}{20}$

**C.** $\dfrac{2}{3} = \dfrac{\square}{6} = \dfrac{6}{\square} = \dfrac{\square}{12} = \dfrac{10}{\square}$

**D.** $\dfrac{3}{4} = \dfrac{6}{\square} = \dfrac{9}{\square} = \dfrac{\square}{\square} = \dfrac{\square}{\square}$

**E.** $\dfrac{4}{5} = \dfrac{\square}{10} \qquad \dfrac{3}{7} = \dfrac{\square}{21} \qquad \dfrac{4}{7} = \dfrac{16}{\square} \qquad \dfrac{3}{4} = \dfrac{21}{\square}$

**F.** $\dfrac{7}{8} = \dfrac{14}{\square} \qquad \dfrac{5}{6} = \dfrac{\square}{18} \qquad \dfrac{2}{7} = \dfrac{12}{\square} \qquad \dfrac{2}{5} = \dfrac{\square}{20}$

**Summer Bridge Math** RB-904087

# Comparing Fractions

Fractions describe equal parts of a whole. They look like this:

 = $\dfrac{1}{2}$ ← part shaded
← total parts

 = $\dfrac{6}{12}$ ← part shaded
← total parts

Larger numbers do not always mean larger fractions. We can compare fractions using <, >, and =.

$\dfrac{1}{3}$ $>$ $\dfrac{1}{6}$

**Study the examples above. Then, write a fraction for each picture.**
**Compare the two fractions using <, >, or = .**

**A.**  ◯

**B.**  ◯

**C.**  ◯

**D.**  ◯

**E.**  ◯

**F.** 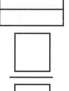 ◯

**Summer Bridge Math** RB-904087

# Adding and Subtracting Fractions

The top and bottom numbers in a fraction have different meanings. They also have different names.

$\dfrac{3}{4}$ ← numerator
← denominator

To add or subtract fractions, the denominators must be the same. The denominator in the answer will also be the same. Add or subtract the numerators only.

$\dfrac{1}{3}$ + $\dfrac{1}{3}$ = $\dfrac{2}{3}$ ← added numerators, 1 + 1
← denominator stays the same

## Study the example above. Then, solve each problem.

**A.** $\dfrac{2}{4} + \dfrac{1}{4} = \dfrac{\Box}{\Box}$ $\qquad$ $\dfrac{6}{8} - \dfrac{4}{8} = \dfrac{\Box}{\Box}$ $\qquad$ $\dfrac{1}{5} + \dfrac{3}{5} = \dfrac{\Box}{\Box}$

**B.** $\dfrac{4}{10} + \dfrac{5}{10} = \dfrac{\Box}{\Box}$ $\qquad$ $\dfrac{7}{8} - \dfrac{5}{8} = \dfrac{\Box}{\Box}$ $\qquad$ $\dfrac{9}{10} - \dfrac{3}{10} = \dfrac{\Box}{\Box}$

**C.** $\dfrac{6}{9} + \dfrac{2}{9} = \dfrac{\Box}{\Box}$ $\qquad$ $\dfrac{42}{100} + \dfrac{36}{100} = \dfrac{\Box}{\Box}$ $\qquad$ $\dfrac{10}{12} - \dfrac{6}{12} = \dfrac{\Box}{\Box}$

**66**

# Improper Fractions

When a fraction, such as $\frac{5}{3}$, has a numerator that is larger than the denominator, it is called an **improper fraction**. The fraction $\frac{3}{3}$ equals 1, so $\frac{5}{3}$ equals 1 and $\frac{2}{3}$. The answer $1\frac{2}{3}$ is called a **mixed number**.

To change an improper fraction to a mixed number, divide the numerator by the denominator and place any remainder as the numerator. $\frac{13}{3} = 13 \div 3 = 4$ with 1 remaining, or $4\frac{1}{3}$.

**Study the examples above. Then, rewrite each fraction as a mixed number.**

**A.** $\frac{14}{3} = $ ___    $\frac{12}{5} = $ ___    $\frac{17}{4} = $ ___    $\frac{13}{2} = $ ___

**B.** $\frac{12}{7} = $ ___    $\frac{18}{5} = $ ___    $\frac{27}{4} = $ ___    $\frac{23}{5} = $ ___

**C.** $\frac{11}{3} = $ ___    $\frac{15}{4} = $ ___    $\frac{24}{5} = $ ___    $\frac{19}{3} = $ ___

**D.** $\frac{38}{4} = $ ___    $\frac{66}{8} = $ ___    $\frac{44}{6} = $ ___    $\frac{84}{9} = $ ___

**E.** $\frac{18}{8} = $ ___    $\frac{26}{6} = $ ___    $\frac{39}{6} = $ ___    $\frac{42}{8} = $ ___

**Summer Bridge Math** RB-904087

# Sequencing Decimals

To sequence **decimals** with **whole numbers,** like 1, 2, and 3, write the whole numbers as decimals. **Example:** 1.0, 2.0, and 3.0. Then, compare the numbers as usual.

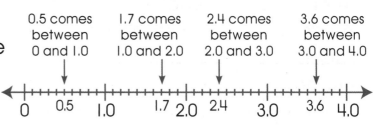

**Study the example above. Then, write the missing numbers.**

**A.**

**B.**

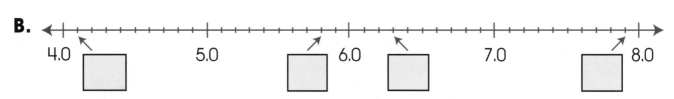

**Write the numbers in order from least to greatest. Imagine a number line to help you.**

**C.**

| 0.1 | 1.6 |
| 0.7 | 1.3 |

→

| | | | |
|---|---|---|---|

**D.**

| 2.4 | 1.9 |
| 0.8 | 0.3 |

→

| | | | |
|---|---|---|---|

**E.**

| 3.6 | 2.8 |
| 3.1 | 0.5 |

→

| | | | |
|---|---|---|---|

**F.**

| 2.6 | 2.1 | 2.8 |
| 1.4 | 0.9 | |

→

| | | | | |
|---|---|---|---|---|

# Using Decimals

Fractions that are **tenths** ($\frac{1}{10}$) or **hundredths** ($\frac{1}{100}$) can be written as decimals. Hint: When there are no whole numbers, put a zero in the ones place.

$\frac{4}{10}$ = four tenths
= 0.4

$1\frac{3}{10}$ = one and three tenths
= 1.3

$\frac{14}{100}$ = fourteen hundredths
= 0.14

$1\frac{23}{100}$ = one and twenty-three hundredths
= 1.23

**Study the examples above. Then, write each fraction problem as a decimal number. Color the balloons with tenths blue. Color the balloons with hundredths green.**

eight tenths =

 =

$\frac{73}{100}$ =

$\frac{36}{100}$ =

$\frac{81}{100}$ =

one tenth =

$\frac{7}{10}$ =

=

$\frac{4}{10}$ =

$\frac{9}{10}$ =

**Summer Bridge Math** RB-904087

# Adding and Subtracting Decimals

To add and subtract decimals, follow these steps:
1. Line up the decimal points.
2. Add or subtract beginning with the column farthest to the right. Regroup if needed.
3. Add or subtract the next column. Regroup if needed.
4. Continue to add or subtract each column, working to the left. Be sure to place the decimal point in your answer.

$$
\begin{array}{r}
3.\overset{5}{\cancel{6}}\overset{1}{6} \\
-\ 0.48 \\
\hline
3.18
\end{array}
\qquad
\begin{array}{r}
\overset{1}{2}.4 \\
+\ 1.8 \\
\hline
4.2
\end{array}
$$

**Study the examples above. Then, solve each problem.**

**A.**
$$
\begin{array}{r} 2.6 \\ +\ 5.6 \\ \hline \end{array}
\qquad
\begin{array}{r} 6.7 \\ -\ 2.9 \\ \hline \end{array}
\qquad
\begin{array}{r} 3.52 \\ +\ 0.78 \\ \hline \end{array}
$$

**B.**
$$
\begin{array}{r} 9.59 \\ +\ 0.18 \\ \hline \end{array}
\qquad
\begin{array}{r} 7.34 \\ -\ 2.16 \\ \hline \end{array}
\qquad
\begin{array}{r} 1.8 \\ +\ 5.9 \\ \hline \end{array}
$$

**C.**
$$
\begin{array}{r} 8.09 \\ +\ 1.36 \\ \hline \end{array}
\qquad
\begin{array}{r} 7.3 \\ -\ 0.9 \\ \hline \end{array}
\qquad
\begin{array}{r} 6.3 \\ -\ 4.8 \\ \hline \end{array}
$$

**D.**
$$
\begin{array}{r} 6.03 \\ +\ 1.81 \\ \hline \end{array}
\qquad
\begin{array}{r} 2.38 \\ -\ 0.16 \\ \hline \end{array}
\qquad
\begin{array}{r} 4.99 \\ -\ 2.83 \\ \hline \end{array}
\qquad
\begin{array}{r} 9.4 \\ -\ 0.7 \\ \hline \end{array}
\qquad
\begin{array}{r} 3.7 \\ +\ 3.9 \\ \hline \end{array}
$$

**Study the examples on page 68. Then, write each fraction as a decimal.**

**A.**  $\dfrac{3}{10}$ = _____     $\dfrac{5}{10}$ = _____     $\dfrac{9}{10}$ = _____     $\dfrac{2}{10}$ = _____

**B.**  $\dfrac{8}{10}$ = _____     $\dfrac{4}{10}$ = _____     $\dfrac{7}{10}$ = _____     $\dfrac{6}{10}$ = _____

**Write each decimal as a fraction.**

**C.**  0.6 = ___     0.4 = ___     0.7 = ___     0.8 = ___

**D.**  0.3 = ___     0.5 = ___     0.2 = ___     0.6 = ___

**Study the examples on pages 67 and 69. Then, write the improper fraction, the mixed number, and the decimal for each problem.**

**E.**

___ or 1 ___ fractions

_____ decimal

**F.**

___ or 1 ___ fractions

_____ decimal

**G.**
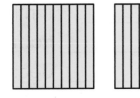

___ or 1 ___ fractions

_____ decimal

**H.**

___ or 1 ___ fractions

_____ decimal

**Summer Bridge Math** RB-904087

# Tenths Practice

**Example:**

| one | tenth |
| --- | --- |
| $\frac{1}{10}$ | fraction |
| 0.1 | decimal |

**Study the examples above and on page 69. Then, write the tenths, the fraction, and the decimal for each problem.**

**A.**
_____ tenths
_____ fraction
_____ decimal

**B.**
_____ tenths
_____ fraction
_____ decimal

**C.**
_____ tenths
_____ fraction
_____ decimal

**D.**
_____ tenths
_____ fraction
_____ decimal

**E.**
_____ tenths
_____ fraction
_____ decimal

**F.**
_____ tenths
_____ fraction
_____ decimal

**G.**
_____ tenths
_____ fraction
_____ decimal

**H.**
_____ tenths
_____ fraction
_____ decimal

**I.** Illustrate $\frac{10}{10}$ or I whole.

_____ tenths
_____ fraction
_____ decimal

# Place Value Practice

Study the examples below. Then, write how many ones, tenths, and hundredths each decimal contains.

|  | | ones | tenths | hundreths |
|---|---|---|---|---|
| | 0.6 | 0 | 6 | 0 |
| A. | 1.07 | | | |
| C. | 5.60 | | | |
| E. | 3.91 | | | |
| G. | 16.06 | | | |
| I. | 0.13 | | | |
| K. | 7.93 | | | |

|  | | ones | tenths | hundreths |
|---|---|---|---|---|
| | 4.3 | 4 | 3 | 0 |
| B. | 3.01 | | | |
| D. | 1.25 | | | |
| F. | 4.11 | | | |
| H. | 2.53 | | | |
| J. | 9.1 | | | |
| L. | 8.84 | | | |

Study the examples below and on pages 69 and 70. Then, solve each problem. Shade in the boxes to show your answer.

0.06 + 0.03 = ___0.09___

**M.** 1.46 + .34 = _____

**N.** 1.5 + 1.7 = _____

**O.** 2.4 + 1.8 = _____

**P.** 0.37 + 2.70 = _____

**Q.** 2.55 + 1.68 = _____

**73**

# Predicting Patterns

By studying a given picture, you can determine its **pattern** and predict what will come next.

**Study the example above. Then, continue each pattern with three more pictures. Use another sheet of paper if you need more room.**

**A.**

**B.**

**C.**

**D.**

**E.**

**F.**

# Number Patterns

**Follow the directions.**

**A.** Skip count by 3. Color all of those numbers red. What pattern do you see?

| 1 | 2 | 3 | 4 | 5 | 6 | 7 | 8 | 9 | 10 |
|---|---|---|---|---|---|---|---|---|---|
| 11 | 12 | 13 | 14 | 15 | 16 | 17 | 18 | 19 | 20 |
| 21 | 22 | 23 | 24 | 25 | 26 | 27 | 28 | 29 | 30 |
| 31 | 32 | 33 | 34 | 35 | 36 | 37 | 38 | 39 | 40 |
| 41 | 42 | 43 | 44 | 45 | 46 | 47 | 48 | 49 | 50 |
| 51 | 52 | 53 | 54 | 55 | 56 | 57 | 58 | 59 | 60 |
| 61 | 62 | 63 | 64 | 65 | 66 | 67 | 68 | 69 | 70 |
| 71 | 72 | 73 | 74 | 75 | 76 | 77 | 78 | 79 | 80 |
| 81 | 82 | 83 | 84 | 85 | 86 | 87 | 88 | 89 | 90 |
| 91 | 92 | 93 | 94 | 95 | 96 | 97 | 98 | 99 | 100 |

**B.** Skip count by 4. Color all of those numbers blue. What pattern do you see?

| 1 | 2 | 3 | 4 | 5 | 6 | 7 | 8 | 9 | 10 |
|---|---|---|---|---|---|---|---|---|---|
| 11 | 12 | 13 | 14 | 15 | 16 | 17 | 18 | 19 | 20 |
| 21 | 22 | 23 | 24 | 25 | 26 | 27 | 28 | 29 | 30 |
| 31 | 32 | 33 | 34 | 35 | 36 | 37 | 38 | 39 | 40 |
| 41 | 42 | 43 | 44 | 45 | 46 | 47 | 48 | 49 | 50 |
| 51 | 52 | 53 | 54 | 55 | 56 | 57 | 58 | 59 | 60 |
| 61 | 62 | 63 | 64 | 65 | 66 | 67 | 68 | 69 | 70 |
| 71 | 72 | 73 | 74 | 75 | 76 | 77 | 78 | 79 | 80 |
| 81 | 82 | 83 | 84 | 85 | 86 | 87 | 88 | 89 | 90 |
| 91 | 92 | 93 | 94 | 95 | 96 | 97 | 98 | 99 | 100 |

**C.** Skip count by 6. Color all of those numbers green. What pattern do you see?

| 1 | 2 | 3 | 4 | 5 | 6 | 7 | 8 | 9 | 10 |
|---|---|---|---|---|---|---|---|---|---|
| 11 | 12 | 13 | 14 | 15 | 16 | 17 | 18 | 19 | 20 |
| 21 | 22 | 23 | 24 | 25 | 26 | 27 | 28 | 29 | 30 |
| 31 | 32 | 33 | 34 | 35 | 36 | 37 | 38 | 39 | 40 |
| 41 | 42 | 43 | 44 | 45 | 46 | 47 | 48 | 49 | 50 |
| 51 | 52 | 53 | 54 | 55 | 56 | 57 | 58 | 59 | 60 |
| 61 | 62 | 63 | 64 | 65 | 66 | 67 | 68 | 69 | 70 |
| 71 | 72 | 73 | 74 | 75 | 76 | 77 | 78 | 79 | 80 |
| 81 | 82 | 83 | 84 | 85 | 86 | 87 | 88 | 89 | 90 |
| 91 | 92 | 93 | 94 | 95 | 96 | 97 | 98 | 99 | 100 |

**D.** Skip count by 11. Color all of those numbers yellow. What pattern do you see?

| 1 | 2 | 3 | 4 | 5 | 6 | 7 | 8 | 9 | 10 |
|---|---|---|---|---|---|---|---|---|---|
| 11 | 12 | 13 | 14 | 15 | 16 | 17 | 18 | 19 | 20 |
| 21 | 22 | 23 | 24 | 25 | 26 | 27 | 28 | 29 | 30 |
| 31 | 32 | 33 | 34 | 35 | 36 | 37 | 38 | 39 | 40 |
| 41 | 42 | 43 | 44 | 45 | 46 | 47 | 48 | 49 | 50 |
| 51 | 52 | 53 | 54 | 55 | 56 | 57 | 58 | 59 | 60 |
| 61 | 62 | 63 | 64 | 65 | 66 | 67 | 68 | 69 | 70 |
| 71 | 72 | 73 | 74 | 75 | 76 | 77 | 78 | 79 | 80 |
| 81 | 82 | 83 | 84 | 85 | 86 | 87 | 88 | 89 | 90 |
| 91 | 92 | 93 | 94 | 95 | 96 | 97 | 98 | 99 | 100 |

**Summer Bridge Math** RB-904087

# Patterns and Functions

Finding patterns is helpful in solving problems. Look at the **number pattern** here. The left column includes the numbers that plug into the brackets [ ] in the "Rule." The right column shows the answers. **Example:** Place 2 (the first number in the left column) in the rule. Then, solve the equation.

[2] x 3 = 6 and 6 + 2 = 8

| Rule: [ ] x 3 + 2 | |
|---|---|
| 2 | 8 |
| 3 | 11 |
| 4 | 14 |
| 5 | 17 |
| 6 | 20 |
| 7 | 23 |
| 8 | 26 |

**Study the example above. Then, look at the pattern. Fill in the chart.**

**A.**

| Rule: [ ] x 2 + 1 | |
|---|---|
| 2 | 5 |
| 3 | 7 |
| 4 | 9 |
| 5 | 11 |
| 6 | |
| 7 | |
| 8 | |

**B.**

| Rule: [ ] x 3 – 2 | |
|---|---|
| 2 | 4 |
| 3 | 7 |
| 4 | 10 |
| 5 | |
| 6 | |
| 7 | |
| 8 | |

**C.**

| Rule: [ ] x 5 + 1 | |
|---|---|
| 2 | 11 |
| 3 | 16 |
| 4 | 21 |
| 5 | |
| 6 | |
| 7 | |
| 8 | |

**D.**

| Rule: [ ] – 2 x 4 | |
|---|---|
| 2 | 0 |
| 3 | 4 |
| 4 | 8 |
| 5 | |
| 6 | |
| 7 | |
| 8 | |

**E. What is the rule?**

| Rule: [ ] x      – | |
|---|---|
| 2 | 0 |
| 3 | 3 |
| 4 | 6 |
| 5 | 9 |
| 6 | 12 |
| 7 | 15 |
| 8 | 18 |

# Shapes

| | |
|---|---|
| **Parallel lines** run side by side and never cross. | A **quadrilateral** is any shape with four sides. |

**Study the shapes. Then, answer each question.**

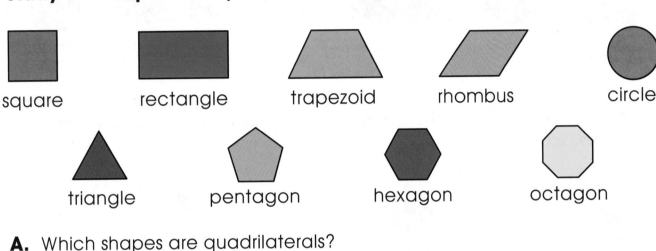

square　　rectangle　　trapezoid　　rhombus　　circle

triangle　　pentagon　　hexagon　　octagon

**A.** Which shapes are quadrilaterals?

_____　　_____

_____　　_____

**B.** What is the only quadrilateral with four equal sides? _____

**C.** What shape has three sides and three angles? _____

**D.** What shape has no sides? _____

**E.** What shape has five sides? _____

**F.** What shape has six sides? _____

**G.** What shape has eight sides? _____

**H.** What shapes have two or more parallel sides?

_____　　_____

_____　　_____

_____

**I.** How is a trapezoid different from a rhombus? _____

_____

　　**Summer Bridge Math** RB-904087

# Spatial Figures

**Spatial figures** are solids that take up space. The flat side of a figure is called a **face**.

cube | sphere | rectangular | cone | pyramid | cylinder
(6 faces) | | prism | (1 face) | (5 faces) | (2 faces)
| | (6 faces) | | |

**Study the figures above. Then, name the spatial figure that each object looks like. Write the number of faces.**

**A.**

_____
# of faces

**B.**

_____
# of faces

**C.**

_____
# of faces

**D.**
_____
# of faces

**E.**

_____
# of faces

**F.**

_____
# of faces

**G.**

_____
# of faces

**H.**

_____
# of faces

**I.**

_____
# of faces

**J.**

_____
# of faces

**K.**

_____
# of faces

# Lines of Symmetry

A **line of symmetry** is a line that divides a figure into two identical parts. These are lines of symmetry:

**Study the examples above. Then, draw 1 line of symmetry for each object.**

**Draw two lines of symmetry for each figure.**

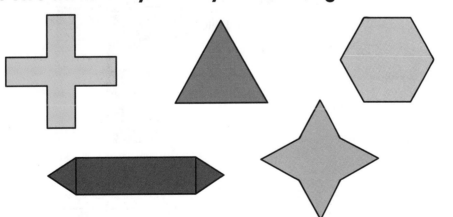

Draw another figure that has two lines of symmetry.

79

# Perimeter

The **perimeter (P)** of a figure is the distance around that figure. The perimeter is measured in units, which may be inches, centimeters, miles, or any other unit of measuring length. To find the perimeter, add all of the sides together.

**Find the perimeter of each figure. Label your answer in the units shown.**

**A.**

8 units

4 units

5 units

7 units

P = _____

**B.**

2 units

1 unit

2 units

1 unit

1 unit

3 units

P = _____

**C.**

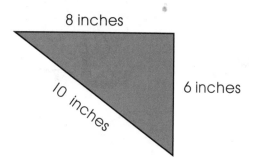

8 inches

10 inches

6 inches

P = _____

**D.**

4 cm

2 cm

4 cm

3 cm

2 cm

1 cm

P = _____

**E.**

7 miles

7 miles

7 miles

P = _____

**F.**

8 miles

2 miles

2 miles

3 miles

3 miles

6 miles

6 miles

2 miles

P = _____

# Exploring Probability

Probability is the chance of something happening. Imagine that you have 6 red apples and 3 green apples. Close your eyes and choose an apple. The probability is higher that you will choose a red apple rather than a green apple. To have equal chances, each choice must have an equal amount.

**Look at the spinners below. Then, answer each question.**

## Spinner A

## Spinner B

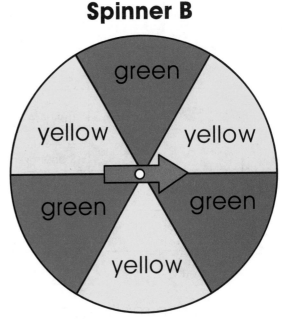

**A.** On Spinner A, would you have more chances of spinning red or blue, or would your chances be equal? _____

**B.** On Spinner B, would you have more chances of spinning yellow or green, or would your chances be equal? _____

**C.** What are the chances of spinning red on Spinner B? _____

**D.** On Spinner A, you have a 2 out of 4 chance of spinning either red or blue. On Spinner B, what chance out of 6 do you have of spinning green? _____

**E.** On Spinner B, what chance out of 6 do you have of spinning yellow?

_____

**Summer Bridge Math** RB-904087

The **title** of a chart tells you what the chart is about.

**Study the chart. Then, answer each question.**

## Wednesday Night Television Schedule

|  | 7:00 | 7:30 | 8:00 | 8:30 | 9:00 | 9:30 | 10:00 | 10:30 |
|---|---|---|---|---|---|---|---|---|
| **2** | Million Dollar Game Show | Jump Start | | News Magazine | | | News | |
| **4** | Lucky Guess | You Should Know | Wednesday Night at the Movies *Friends Forever* | | | | News | |
| **5** | Best Friends | Sarah's Secret | Where They Are | Time to Hope | Tom's Talk Show | | News | |
| **7** | Freakin' Out | Lost Alone | Last One Standing | Sports Tonight | | | News | |
| **11** | Your Health | Eating Right | Nutrition News | | Cooking with Kate | | Home Decorating | Shopping Show |
| **24** | Silly Rabbit | Clyde the Clown | Your Lucky Day | Slime & Rhyme | Cartoon Alley | | Fun Times | Make Me Laugh |

**A.** What information does this chart give?_____

_____

**B.** What time is *Slime & Rhyme* on Channel 24? _____

**C.** What channel is *Tom's Talk Show* on at 9:00? _____

**D.** What show is on Channel 11 at 7:30? _____

**E.** How long is the Wednesday night movie on Channel 4? _____

**F.** On how many channels can you watch news at 10:00?_____

**G.** How many shows start at 8:00? _____

**H.** What would you choose to watch at 9:00? _____

# Interpreting Graphs and Grids

The **line graph** below shows points of information. Lines are then drawn between the **points** to make an easy comparison. This line graph shows the temperature change throughout one week.

**Study the graph below. Then, answer each question.**

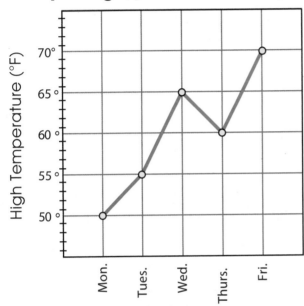

**A.** What was the difference in temperature from Wednesday to Friday? _____

**B.** How many degrees did the temperature drop from Wednesday to Thursday? _____

**C.** What was the lowest temperature reading? _____ °F

**D.** What was the difference in temperature from Monday to Thursday? _____

This is a **coordinate grid**. It is used to show the location of something. The numbers along the bottom and side describe the location using an ordered pair. The first number is from the bottom of the grid, and the second number is from the side of the grid. For example, the raindrop is found at (6, 3). Can you find it?

**Draw the symbols found at:**

**E.** (2, 3) _____

**F.** (4, 1) _____

**G.** (3, 5) _____

**H.** Write each ordered pair.

© Rainbow Bridge Publishing

**Summer Bridge Math** RB-904087

# Addition and Subtraction

Problem solving means using the numbers in a story to solve a math problem.

**Example:** John ate 12 grapes. Then, he ate 10 more. How many grapes did he eat in all? 12 + 10 = 22, so John ate 22 grapes.

## Study the example above. Then, solve each problem.

**A.** Anthony made 9 clay pots. He broke 4 of the pots. How many pots does he have left?

**B.** Keenan had 17 boxes of candy to sell. He sold 2 boxes to his grandma. His dad sold 9 boxes to people at work. How many more boxes did Keenan have to sell?

**C.** Min collects trading cards. She wants to collect all 15 cards in a series. She already has 8 of the cards. How many more cards does Min need?

**D.** Trina had 7 fish in her aquarium. She bought 4 more fish. How many fish does she have altogether?

**E.** Nina got 16 pieces of candy from the piñata. She ate 7 pieces. How many does she have left?

**F.** Bradley read 5 books the first month of summer break and 8 books the second month. How many books did he read in all?

# Three-Digit Addition and Subtraction

Read the problems carefully. Look for the key words to help you know whether to add or subtract to find the answer.

| **Add** | **Subtract** |
|---|---|
| how many in all | how many more |
| how many together | how many left |

**Study the key words above and the example on page 84. Then, solve each problem.**

**A.** Anthony had 348 pennies. His brother had 239. How many more pennies did Anthony have than his brother?

**B.** Celeste collected 479 aluminum cans. Nicole collected 742 cans. How many cans did the girls collect altogether?

**C.** The electronics store had 371 televisions in stock. They sold 138 on the weekend. How many televisions do they have left?

**D.** My big brother Matt weighs 189 pounds. His friend weighs 202 pounds. How much less does Matt weigh than his friend?

**E.** The school library has 879 nonfiction books and 932 fiction books. How many books does the library have altogether?

**F.** The girls earned 487 points for selling cookies. The boys earned 399 points. How many more points did the girls earn than the boys?

**Summer Bridge Math** RB-904087

# Multiplication

Some story problems can be answered using multiplication. They ask you to find a total number, similar to addition. The difference is that these stories involve equal sets.

**Example:** Matthew ordered 3 ice cream cones. Each cone had 2 scoops. How many scoops of ice cream did Matthew order?

$$3 \quad x \quad 2 \quad = \quad 6$$

| number of sets | number in each set | total scoops ordered |
|:---:|:---:|:---:|

**Study the example above. Then, solve each problem. Show your work.**

**A.** Tina rode her bike 17 miles each day for 6 days. How many miles did Tina ride?

**B.** Jack read 7 books. Each book had 48 pages. How many pages did Jack read?

**C.** Marissa has 5 trading card books. Each book has 50 cards in it. How many trading cards does Marissa have?

**D.** Juan put his stamp collection into 4 boxes. He put 73 stamps in each box. How many stamps does he have?

**Summer Bridge Math** RB-904087

# Choosing the Operation

**Study the examples on pages 84 and 86. Then, solve each problem.**

**A.** Bev's 3 guinea pigs ate 24 seeds each. How many seeds did the guinea pigs eat?

**B.** We found 6 spider webs. Each web had trapped 17 bugs. How many bugs were trapped?

**C.** A ticket to the game costs $26.00. Amy has $18.00. How much more does Amy need to buy a ticket?

**D.** Haley has 52 dimes in her bank. She has 39 nickels. How many coins does she have?

**E.** We passed 8 trucks on the highway. Each truck honked 4 times. How many honks did the trucks make in all?

**F.** Jon is making lemonade for 16 people. Each glass needs 3 spoons of powdered mix. How many spoons of lemonade mix will Jon use?

# Division

> Other story problems can be answered using division. They ask you to find missing parts or make smaller groups. They also involve making equal sets.
>
> **Example:** Yasmine had 9 hair ribbons. She split them evenly between 3 friends. How many ribbons did each friend get?
>
>
>
> $$9 \div 3 = 3$$
> total ribbons    number of groups    ribbons each

**Study the example above. Then, solve each problem. Show your work.**

**A.** The Millers have 6 children. When they come to the pool, they bring 36 toys to share equally among the children. How many toys does each child get?

**B.** Mrs. Weitz passed out 24 papers equally to 8 students. How many papers did each student get?

**C.** Tara and Sira share 12 cookies evenly. How many cookies does each girl get?

**D.** There are 88 total horse legs in the pasture. How many horses are there?

# Division with Remainders

Sometimes, objects do not divide evenly into groups. There will be objects left over.

**Example:** There are 11 cookies. There are 3 children. How many cookies will each child get? How many cookies will be left over?

Each child gets 3 cookies. There are 2 cookies left over.

**Study the example above. Then, solve each problem.**

**A.** There are 14 pieces of paper. Miss Scriber places them in 3 equal stacks.

How many papers are in each stack? _____

How many papers are left over?

_____

**B.** Mark has 15 books. He put them on 2 shelves, with the same number of books on each shelf.

How many books are on each shelf? _____

How many books are left over?

_____

**C.** Alex has 11 apples. He needs 5 apples to make a pie. How many pies can he make?

_____

How many apples are left over?

_____

**D.** Jenny has 19 walnuts. She wants to divide them evenly between 3 bags.

How many walnuts will be in each bag? _____

How many walnuts are left over? _____

# Time

A.M. refers to the morning time from 12:00 midnight until 12:00 noon. P.M. refers to the afternoon and evening time from 12:00 noon until 12:00 midnight. There are 60 minutes in one hour.

**Solve each problem. Refer to the clock above if you need help.**

**A.** Isabella wants to watch a show at 8:00 P.M. It is 7:23 P.M. How many more minutes is it until the show starts?

**B.** Cade's favorite show starts at 7:30 P.M. It is 90 minutes long. What time will the show end?

**C.** Taylor's favorite show started at 4:30 P.M. It is 30 minutes long. It is 4:53 P.M. right now. How many more minutes is the show on?

**D.** Melissa watched a movie that started at 7:00 P.M. It lasted 1 hour and 47 minutes. What time did the movie end?

**E.** Jonathan started watching a show at 4:16 P.M. He turned the television off at 5:37 P.M. How long did he watch television?

**F.** Chelsea watched 2 30-minute shows on Monday, 1 30-minute show on Wednesday, and 3 30-minute shows on Friday. How many hours of television did she watch that week?

# Money

Mike wants to buy a game that costs $23.00. He has saved $17.00. How much more does he need to save?

Subtract $17.00 from $23.00 to find out how much more. Mike needs to save $6.00 more.

$$\begin{array}{r} \$23.00 \\ -\ \$17.00 \\ \hline \$\ \ 6.00 \end{array}$$

## Study the example above. Then, solve each problem.

**A.** Gina had $17.22. She earned $5.00 more for helping her mother. How much money does Gina have now?

**B.** Matt had $18.77. He wanted to buy a CD for $14.50. How much would he have left if he bought the CD?

**C.** Josh got $3.50 from his mother, $4.00 from his father, and $10.00 from his grandparents. How much money did Josh get?

**D.** Len had $53.00. He was trying to earn enough money for a bike that cost $87.00. How much more money does he need?

**E.** Dan earned $20.00 for mowing the neighbor's yard. He already had $12.00. How much money does he have now?

**F.** Emma wanted to buy a science kit that cost $18.00. She only had $6.00. How much more money does she need?

# Problem Solving Using Charts

Sometimes a story problem can be answered by writing the information in a chart.

**Example:** By the end of 1 week, the grass in Mr. Johnson's yard had grown to 3 inches. After 2 weeks, the grass was 6 inches high. If the pattern continues, how tall will Mr. Johnson's grass be after 6 weeks? Follow these steps:

1. Fill in the information from the story.
2. Figure out the pattern.
3. Complete the chart using the pattern.

| Week # | 1 | 2 | 3 | 4 | 5 | 6 |
|--------|---|---|---|----|----|----|
| Inches | 3 | 6 | 9 | 12 | 15 | 18 |

Mr Johnson's grass will be 18 inches tall after 6 weeks.

**Study the example above. Then, complete each chart to solve the problem. Circle your answer in the chart.**

**A.** Sparky likes to run around the house. It takes him 4 minutes to make it around 2 times. How long will it take Sparky to run around 10 times?

| # of times | | | | | | | | | | |
|------------|---|---|---|---|---|---|---|---|---|---|
| # of minutes | | | | | | | | | | |

**B.** Patsy spends 3 hours every 2 days practicing her flute. After 4 days she has spent 6 hours practicing. How many hours will she practice in 12 days?

| # of days | | | | | | | | | | |
|-----------|---|---|---|---|---|---|---|---|---|---|
| # of hours | | | | | | | | | | |

# Answer Key

**Page 7:** ON HIS FEET!

**Page 8: A.** 6,911; **B.** 4,073; **C.** 9,207; **D.** 839; **E.** 9,601; **F.** 8,390; **G.** 417; **H.** 5,082; **I.** 470; **J.** 3,512; **K.** 6,914; **L.** 4,413

**Page 9: A.** three hundred forty-seven; **B.** two hundred seventy-nine; **C.** nine hundred sixty; **D.** seven hundred nineteen; **E.** eight hundred one; **F.** five hundred ninety; **G.** one hundred thirty-five; **H.** five hundred nine; **I.** six hundred eighty; **J.** nine hundred ninety-nine; **K.** 313; **L.** 809; **M.** 426; **N.** 211; **O.** 751; **P.** 105; **Q.** 532; **R.** 944

**Page 10: A.** 5th, 6th, 7th, 8th, 9th, 10th; **B.** 21st, 22nd, 23rd, 24th, 26th, 27th; **C.** 80th, 81st, 82nd, 84th, 85th, 86th, 87th; **D.** 7; **E.** 5; **F.** 12th

**Page 11: A.** 1, 3, 4, 5; 1,345 **B.** 2, 1, 6, 1; 2,161; **C.** 1, 0, 3, 0; 1,030; **D.** 3, 1, 0, 0; 3,100; **E.** 2, 4, 4, 0; 2,440; **F.** 1, 2, 1, 3; 1,213

**Page 12: A.** 0, 5, 7, 3, 9; **B.** 1, 4, 6, 5, 0; **C.** 2, 7, 3, 8, 1; **D.** 4, 0, 7, 3, 6; **E.** 9, 1, 4, 7, 5; **F.** 5, 5, 8, 3, 7; **G.** 8, 6, 9, 0, 2; **H.** 0, 4, 5, 6, 0; **I.** 3, 1, 0, 4, 8; **J.** 1, 1, 1, 1, 1; **K.** 7, 9, 2, 7, 7; **L.** 6, 8, 5, 9, 3; **M.** 9, 9, 9, 9, 9; **N.** 4, 8, 3, 0, 5; **O.** hundreds, hundreds; **P.** thousands, ten thousands; **Q.** ten thousands, tens; **R.** tens, ten thousands; **S.** hundreds, thousands; **T.** ones, tens; **U.** tens, ones; **V.** ten thousands, ten thousands; **W.** thousands, hundreds

**Page 13: A.** 9,000 + 500 + 10 + 6; **B.** 2,000 + 300 + 50 + 8; **C.** 1,000 + 400 + 0 + 7; **D.** 0 + 900 + 20 + 1; **E.** 7,000 + 800 + 0 + 0; **F.** 3,000 + 200 + 60 + 4; **G.** 5,000 + 100 + 80 + 2; **H.** 0 + 600 + 10 + 4; **I.** 4,000 + 0 + 70 + 3; **J.** 9,000 + 500 + 30 + 0

**Page 14: A.** 1,533; **B.** 5,947; **C.** 3,755; **D.** 7,479; **E.** 9,021; **F.** 3,102; **G.** 3,506; **H.** 6,098; **I.** 3,609; **J.** 1,698; **K.** 3,000 + 400 + 50 + 6; **L.** 7,000 + 300 + 20 + 4; **M.** 9,000 + 100 + 50 + 2; **N.** 3,000 + 500 + 60 + 9; **O.** 2,000 + 400 + 30 + 1; **P.** 4,000 + 0 + 20 + 2

**Page 15: A.** >; **B.** >; **C.** <; **D.** =; **E.** <; **F.** >; **G.** <; **H.** <; **I.** =; **J.** <

**Page 16: A.** 149; **B.** 566; **C.** 430; **D.** 390; **E.** 804; **F.** 981; **G.** 709; **H.** 871; **I.** 990; **J.** 805; **K.** <, >; **L.** <, >; **M.** <, <; **N.** >, <; **O.** >, <; **P.** >, <; **Q.** >, <; **R.** >, <; **S.** <, <

**Page 17:** From top to bottom and left to right: 100, 600, 300, 700, 900, 700, 500, 900

**Page 18: A.** 0, 4, 8, 12; **B.** 0, 6, 12; **C.** 33, 36, 39, 42, 45; **D.** 62, 64, 66, 68, 70, 72, 74; **E.** 84, 88, 92, 96

**Page 19: A.** 65, 89, 78, 58, 85, 69; **B.** 99, 93, 97, 99, 59, 89; **C.** 89, 96, 78, 79, 59, 59; **D.** 87, 99, 96, 89, 87, 71; **E.** 88, 85, 67, 78, 79, 86; **F.** 86, 79, 49, 99, 85, 74

**Page 20: A.** 51, 92, 81, 86, 64, 90; **B.** 94, 130, 92, 92, 103, 75; **C.** 92, 111, 70, 114, 130, 140; **D.** 81, 83, 83, 61, 46, 86; **E.** 70, 62, 96, 90, 81, 76

**Page 21: A.** 885, 778, 988, 998, 527; **B.** 594, 986, 969, 789, 919; **C.** 788, 985, 867, 877, 798; **D.** 786, 786, 879, 769, 888; **E.** 985, 678, 899, 957, 898; **F.** 956, 699, 969, 889, 859

**Page 22: A.** 451, 702, 816, 1,192, 830; **B.** 823, 851; 1,044; 1,013; 605; **C.** 900, 813; 1,011; 1,177; 1,021; **D.** 613, 821, 862, 750, 929; **E.** 1,180; 1,405; 872, 894, 831; **F.** 1,174; 974, 611, 794, 890

**Page 23: A.** 8,500; 6,712; 9,809; 9,080; 4,401; **B.** 6,308; 13,046; 8,180; 11,055; 9,742; **C.** 8,066; 11,195; 10,191; 9,809; 11,207; **D.** 11,906; 7,600; 7,424; 11,039; 10,889; **E.** 5,008; 10,087; 6,041; 11,817; 11,817; **F.** 12,570; 7,715; 5,026; 6,102; 12,079

**Page 24: A.** 6, 7, 9, 10, 11, 11, 12; **B.** 12, 10, 13, 14, 7, 10, 12; **C.** 13, 13, 11, 15, 17, 14, 18; **D.** 13, 15, 15, 18, 18, 18, 13; **E.** 16, 17, 17, 18, 18, 13, 18

**Page 25: A.** $11.37, $12.23; **B.** $13.50, $16.53, $10.58; **C.** $13.34, $18.08, $19.04; **D.** $6.63, $12.70; The left castle is located in the richest kingdom.

**Page 26: A.** 54, 40, 22, 65, 61, 15; **B.** 26, 20, 24, 23, 51, 50; **C.** 32, 23, 4, 60, 24, 24; **D.** 22, 10, 40, 15, 26, 16; **E.** 72, 41, 50, 34, 41, 63

**Page 27: A.** 19, 79, 19, 26, 16, 49; **B.** 19, 58, 14, 59, 28, 32; **C.** 28, 68, 36, 39, 14, 47; **D.** 25, 39, 59, 38, 48, 24; **E.** 38, 29, 49, 8, 58, 19

**Page 28: A.** 431, 213, 225, 236, 223; **B.** 553, 322, 812, 121, 205; **C.** 63, 137, 462, 414, 142; **D.** 633, 342, 704, 312, 148; **E.** 220, 414, 260, 316, 541

**Page 29: A.** 699, 269, 469, 429, 257; **B.** 187, 292, 739, 289, 228; **C.** 424, 338, 429, 449, 608; **D.** 584, 193, 691, 84, 470

# Answer Key

**Page 30: A.** 4,406; 1,296; 2,067; 2,947; 2,087; **B.** 4,728; 6,035; 3,760; 5,965; 1,082; **C.** 3,559; 5,032; 4,802; 2,058; 2,758; **D.** 909; 4,063; 1,879; 6,077; 7,367; **E.** 3,696; 4,086; 1,274; 4,663; 4,977

**Page 31: A.** 2,338; 3,729; 1,589; 3,820; **B.** 8,858; 2,612; 8,768; 485; **C.** 3,805; 7,388; 5,321; 458; **D.** 774; 2,479

**Page 32: A.** 58, 66, 28, 71, 92; **B.** 24, 59, 19, 81, 32; **C.** 60, 142, 12, 57, 92; **D.** 33, 85, 18, 87, 61; **E.** 39, 47, 19, 92, 89; **F.** 113, 74, 19, 82, 16

**Page 33: A.** 1,025; 307; 1,226; 1,012; 462; **B.** 732, 921, 118; 1,119; 349; **C.** 198, 822, 438; 1,381; 463; **D.** 823, 652, 507, 920, 508; **E.** 426, 459; 1,082; 1,024; 865; **F.** 1,234; 394, 831, 904, 928

**Page 34:** clockwise from the top: 240, 600, 350, 342, 999, 785

**Page 35: A.** 5 + 5 + 5 = 15, 3 x 5 = 15; **B.** 3 + 3 = 6, 2 x 3 = 6; **C.** 2 + 2 + 2 + 2 = 8, 4 x 2 = 8; **D.** 4 + 4 = 8, 2 x 4 = 8; **E.** 3 + 3 + 3 = 9, 3 x 3 = 9; **F.** 4 + 4 + 4 = 12, 3 x 4 = 12; **G.** 2 + 2 + 2 = 6, 3 x 2 = 6; **H.** 5 + 5 = 10, 2 x 5 = 10

**Page 36: Row 1:** 2, 3, 4, 5, 6, 7, 8, 9; **Row 2:** 2, 4, 6, 8, 10, 12, 14, 16, 18; **Row 3:** 3, 6, 9, 12, 15, 18, 21, 24, 27; **Row 4:** 4, 8, 12, 16, 20, 24, 28, 32, 36; **Row 5:** 5, 10, 15, 20, 25, 30, 35, 40, 45; **Row 6:** 6, 12, 18, 24, 30, 36, 42, 48, 54; **Row 7:** 7, 14, 21, 28, 35, 42, 49, 56, 63; **Row 8:** 8, 16, 24, 32, 40, 48, 56, 64, 72; **Row 9:** 9, 18, 27, 36, 45, 54, 63, 72, 81; **A.** the number; **B.** They are all even numbers.; **C.** They end in 0 or 5.; **D.** 9; **E.** 12

**Page 37: 1st riddle:** YOUR RIGHT ELBOW!; **2nd riddle:** BECAUSE FISH HAVE THEIR OWN SCALES!

**Page 38: A.** 4, 6, 15, 6, 12; **B.** 16, 10, 12, 8, 2; **C.** 14, 18, 18, 16, 20; **D.** 27, 30, 24, 21, 24; **E.** 16, 30, 40, 63, 64; **F.** 20, 72, 42, 35, 32; **G.** 36, 28, 56, 81, 36; **H.** 20, 25, 45, 48, 28

**Page 39: A.** 48, 22, 26, 39; **B.** 33, 28, 36, 44; **C.** 13, 66, 66, 64; **D.** 84, 48, 44, 63; **E.** 99, 96, 93, 62

**Page 40: A.** 90, 70, 91, 72, 110; **B.** 84, 100, 192, 161, 112; **C.** 78, 312, 220, 204, 117; **D.** 252, 270, 288, 112, 56; **E.** 210, 126, 154, 170, 141; **F.** 38, 198, 336, 252, 415

**Page 41: A.** 2,488; 496, 900, 849, 1,998; 548; **B.** 1,001; 645, 824, 750, 927, 832; **C.** 3,609; 840, 756, 1,200; 888; 3,647; **D.** 3,699; 3,102; 864, 648, 408; 3,570; **E.** 6,349; 970, 2,439; 5,632; 672; 1,175; **F.** 1,086; 1,000; 1,688; 5,346; 963; 3,950

**Page 42: A.** $36.50, $27.28, $24.72, $43.05; **B.** $1.36, $7.92, $21.72, $14.95; **C.** $9.59, $8.19, $32.00, $11.07; **D.** $0.88, $11.46, $2.96, $47.60

**Page 43: A.** five groups of two circled, 2; **B.** three groups of five circled, 5; **C.** three groups of two circled, 2; **D.** two groups of four circled, 4; **E.** three groups of three circled, 3; **F.** four groups of three circled, 3; **G.** six groups of two circled, 2; **H.** three groups of six circled, 6; **I.** seven groups of two circled, 2

**Page 44:** All groups in each problem should have an equal number of objects drawn. **A.** 21 ÷ 3 = 7; **B.** 30 ÷ 5 = 6; **C.** 36 ÷ 9 = 4; **D.** 18 ÷ 6 = 3

**Page 45:** All groups in each problem should have the same number of objects drawn. **A.** 6; **B.** 4; **C.** 3; **D.** 4; **E.** 2; **F.** 6

**Page 46: A.** 6, 6, 7, 9; **B.** 7, 7, 9, 9; **C.** 7, 9, 9, 7; **D.** 6, 4, 8, 6; **E.** 4, 7, 5, 8; **F.** 4, 6, 5, 6; **G.** 7, 8, 4, 8; **H.** 8, 3, 9, 9

**Page 47: A.** 7 r1, 5 r2, 4 r3, 3 r4; **B.** 6 r1, 3 r3, 3 r2, 5 r3; **C.** 7 r7, 9 r1, 5 r1, 4 r4; **D.** 4 r2, 2 r1, 3 r1, 6 r2; **E.** 4 r1, 3 r4, 4 r6, 4 r6; **F.** 3 r4, 2 r4, 2 r1, 5 r2

**Page 48: A.** 3, 3, 3, 4, 4; **B.** 8, 7, 7, 8, 7; **C.** 6 r1, 3 r3, 3 r3, 3 r1, 3 r2; **D.** 6 r1, 5 r4, 3 r1, 5 r2, 8 r2; **E.** 9, 6, 8, 6, 6; **F.** 17 r1, 19 r5, 3 r2, 9 r3, 5 r1

**Page 49: A.** 4, 4; **B.** 3, 3; **C.** 4, 4; **D.** 5, 5; **E.** 5, 5; **F.** 3, 3; **G.** 3, 3; **H.** 6, 6; **I.** 5, 5; **J.** 9, 9; **K.** 5, 5; **L.** 2, 2; **M.** 4, 4; **N.** 2, 2; **O.** 6, 6

**Page 50:** Answers may be in a different order. **A.** 6 x 7 = 42, 7 x 6 = 42, 42 ÷ 7 = 6, 42 ÷ 6 = 7; **B.** 4 x 5 = 20, 5 x 4 = 20, 20 ÷ 5 = 4, 20 ÷ 4 = 5; **C.** 9 x 8 = 72, 8 x 9 = 72, 72 ÷ 8 = 9, 72 ÷ 9 = 8; **D.** 7 x 8 = 56, 8 x 7 = 56, 56 ÷ 8 = 7, 56 ÷ 7 = 8

**Page 51: A.** 48, 21, 16, 36, 14; **B.** 36, 24, 16, 12, 15; **C.** 64, 30, 6, 28, 18; **D.** 30, 56, 20, 49, 72; **E.** 9, 5, 8, 8; **F.** 9, 6, 7, 7; **G.** 8, 6, 3, 7; **H.** 5, 9, 8, 4

**Page 52: A.** 6:30, 11:00, 5:00; **B.** 6:00, 12:30, 10:30

**Page 53: A.** 30, 10:00, 10:30; **B.** 15, 2:00, 2:15; **C.** 35, 7:00, 7:35; **D.** 55, 9:00, 9:55; **E.** 10, 8:00, 8:10; **F.** 50, 4:00, 4:50; **G.** 5, 10:00, 10:05; **H.** 45, 6:00, 6:45; **I.** 30, 5:00, 5:30; **J.** 5, 12:00, 12:05

# Answer Key

**A.**  **B.**

**C.**  **D.**

**E.**  **F.**

**G.**  **H.**

**I.**

**Page 55: A.** 82¢; **B.** 43¢; **C.** 95¢; **D.** 81¢; **E.** 85¢; **F.** 86¢; **G.** 29¢; **H.** 45¢

**Page 56: A.** 25, 25, 10, 10, 10, 10, 5, 5, 100¢; **B.** 50, 10, 5, 5, 5, 1, 1, 1, 78¢; **C.** 50, 10, 10, 10, 5, 5, 1, 1, 92¢; **D.** 25, 25, 10, 5, 5, 5, 1, 1, 77¢; **E.** 50, 25, 5, 5, 1, 1, 1, 1, 89¢; **F.** 25, 25, 25, 10, 5, 5, 5, 1, 101¢

**Page 57: A.** $1.55; **B.** $2.48; **C.** $7.45; **D.** $10.85; **E.** $17.17; **F.** $69.00

**Page 58: A.** $3.90; **B.** $3.80; **C.** $4.05; **D.** $5.40; **E.** $0.50; **F.** $4.05; **G.** $0.85; **H.** $15.00; **I.** $0.81; **J.** $0.05; **K.** $2.51; **L.** $0.77

**Page 59: A.** 6 feet; **B.** 9 inches; **C.** 1 inch; **D.** 20 inches; **E.** 2 inches; **F.** 1 inch; **G.** 2, 2, 1, 1, 6 inches

**Page 60: A.** 124, 4; **B.** 12, 1, 6; **C.** 36, 2, 2; **D.** 200, 4,000, 3; **E.** <, >; **F.** <, >; **G.** >, =; **H.** =, >

**Page 61:** from left to right and top to bottom: 2 ounces, 5 grams, 18 kilograms, 105 pounds, 38 ounces, 26 pounds

**Page 62: A.** <, =, >; **B.** <, <, <; **C.** =, >, =; **D.** 85, 30, Answers will vary, but accept any answers that include warm-weather attire.; **E.** 32, 0, Answers will vary, but accept any answers that include cold-weather attire.

**Page 63: A.** $\frac{1}{6}$; **B.** $\frac{3}{8}$; **C.** $\frac{3}{4}$; **D.** $\frac{5}{8}$; **E.** $\frac{7}{9}$; **F.** $\frac{7}{12}$

**Page 64: A.** 2, 3, 12, 15; **B.** 2, 3, 16, 5; **C.** 4, 9, 8, 15; **D.** 8, 12, $\frac{12}{16}$, $\frac{15}{20}$; **E.** 8, 9, 28, 28; **F.** 16, 15, 42, 8

**Page 65: A.** $\frac{1}{3} < \frac{2}{3}$; **B.** $\frac{2}{4} = \frac{4}{8}$; **C.** $\frac{3}{8} < \frac{1}{2}$; **D.** $\frac{1}{3} = \frac{2}{6}$; **E.** $\frac{3}{4} > \frac{2}{4}$; **F.** $\frac{1}{2} < \frac{3}{4}$

**Page 66: A.** $\frac{3}{4}$, $\frac{2}{8}$, $\frac{4}{5}$; **B.** $\frac{9}{10}$, $\frac{2}{8}$, $\frac{6}{10}$; **C.** $\frac{8}{9}$, $\frac{78}{100}$, $\frac{4}{12}$

**Page 67: A.** $4\frac{2}{3}$, $2\frac{2}{5}$, $4\frac{1}{4}$, $6\frac{1}{2}$; **B.** $1\frac{5}{7}$, $3\frac{3}{5}$, $6\frac{3}{4}$, $4\frac{3}{5}$; **C.** $3\frac{2}{3}$, $3\frac{3}{4}$, $4\frac{4}{5}$, $9\frac{1}{3}$; **D.** $9\frac{2}{4}$, $8\frac{2}{8}$, $7\frac{2}{6}$, $9\frac{3}{9}$; **E.** $2\frac{2}{8}$, $4\frac{2}{6}$, $6\frac{3}{8}$, $5\frac{2}{8}$

**Page 68: A.** 0.5, 1.4, 2.8, 3.7; **B.** 4.1, 5.8, 6.3, 7.9; **C.** 0.1, 0.7, 1.3, 1.6; **D.** 0.3, 0.8, 1.9, 2.4; **E.** 0.5, 2.8, 3.1, 3.6; **F.** 0.9, 1.4, 2.1, 2.6, 2.8

**Page 69: blue:** 0.8, 0.1, 0.7, 0.6, 0.4, 0.9; **green:** 0.15, 0.73, 0.36, 0.81

**Page 70: A.** 8.2, 3.8, 4.3; **B.** 9.77, 5.18, 7.7; **C.** 9.45, 6.4, 1.5; **D.** 7.84, 2.22, 2.16, 8.7, 7.6

**Page 71: A.** 0.3, 0.5, 0.9, 0.2; **B.** 0.8, 0.4, 0.7, 0.6; **C.** $\frac{6}{10}$, $\frac{4}{10}$, $\frac{7}{10}$, $\frac{8}{10}$; **D.** $\frac{3}{10}$, $\frac{5}{10}$, $\frac{2}{10}$, $\frac{6}{10}$; **E.** $\frac{13}{10}$, $1\frac{3}{10}$, 1.3; **F.** $\frac{16}{10}$, $1\frac{6}{10}$, 1.6; **G.** $\frac{18}{10}$, $1\frac{8}{10}$, 1.8; **H.** $\frac{20}{10}$, $1\frac{10}{10}$, 2.0

**Page 72: A.** seven, $\frac{7}{10}$, 0.7; **B.** two, $\frac{2}{10}$, 0.2; **C.** five, $\frac{5}{10}$, 0.5; **D.** four, $\frac{4}{10}$, 0.4; **E.** three, $\frac{3}{10}$, 0.3; **F.** eight, $\frac{8}{10}$, 0.8; **G.** nine, $\frac{9}{10}$, 0.9; **H.** six, $\frac{6}{10}$, 0.6; **I.** ten, $\frac{10}{10}$, 1.0; The whole box should be shaded.

**Page 73: A.** 1, 0, 7; **B.** 3, 0, 1; **C.** 5, 6, 0; **D.** 1, 2, 5; **E.** 3, 9, 1; **F.** 4, 1, 1; **G.** 16, 0, 6; **H.** 2, 5, 3; **I.** 0, 1, 3; **J.** 9, 1, 0; **K.** 7, 9, 3; **L.** 8, 8, 4; **M.** 1.80; **N.** 3.2; **O.** 4.2; **P.** 3.07; **Q.** 4.23; Boxes should be shaded correctly.

**Page 74:**
**A.**

**Summer Bridge Math** RB-904087

# Answer Key

**Page 75: A.** 3, 6, 9, 12, 15, 18, 21, 24, 27, 30, 33, 36, 39, 42, 45, 48, 51, 54, 57, 60, 63, 66, 69, 72, 75, 78, 81, 84, 87, 90, 93, 96, 99; **B.** 4, 8, 12, 16, 20, 24, 28, 32, 36, 40, 44, 48, 52, 56, 60, 64, 68, 72, 76, 80, 84, 88, 92, 96, 100; **C.** 6, 12, 18, 24, 30, 36, 42, 48, 54, 60, 66, 72, 78, 84, 90, 96; **D.** 11, 22, 33, 44, 55, 66, 77, 88, 99; Other answers will vary.

**Page 76: A.** 13, 15, 17; **B.** 13, 16, 19, 22; **C.** 26, 31, 36, 41; **D.** 12, 16, 20, 24; **E.** [ ] x 3 – 6

**Page 77: A.** square, rhombus, rectangle, trapezoid; **B.** square; **C.** triangle; **D.** circle; **E.** pentagon; **F.** hexagon; **G.** octagon; **H.** square, rhombus, rectangle, hexagon, trapezoid, octagon; **I.** Answers will vary but may include a trapezoid has one pair of parallel sides, but a rhombus has two pairs of parallel sides.

**Page 78: A.** cone, 1; **B.** cylinder, 2; **C.** sphere, 0; **D.** rectangular prism, 6; **E.** pyramid, 5; **F.** cube, 6; **G.** cylinder, 2; **H.** sphere, 0; **I.** pyramid, 5; **J.** cone, 1; **K.** rectangular prism, 6

**Page 79:** Lines of symmetry should be drawn correctly.

**Page 80: A.** 24 units; **B.** 10 units; **C.** 24 inches; **D.** 16 cm; **E.** 21 miles; **F.** 32 miles

**Page 81: A.** equal; **B.** equal; **C.** none; **D.** 3; **E.** 3

**Page 82: A.** the times and channels of Wednesday night television programs; **B.** 8:30 P.M.; **C.** 5; **D.** *Eating Right*; **E.** 2 hours; **F.** 4; **G.** 5; **H.** Answers will vary.

**Page 83: A.** 6 degrees; **B.** 5 degrees; **C.** 10; **D.** 11; **E.**  **F.** ◯ **G.** ◔ **H.** (1, 1), (0, 4)

**Page 84: A.** 5 pots; **B.** 6 boxes; **C.** 7 cards; **D.** 11 fish; **E.** 9 pieces of candy; **F.** 13 books

**Page 85: A.** 109 pennies; **B.** 1,221 cans; **C.** 233 televisions; **D.** 13 pounds; **E.** 1,811 books; **F.** 88 points

**Page 86: A.** 102 miles; **B.** 336 pages; **C.** 250 trading cards; **D.** 292 stamps

**Page 87: A.** 72 seeds; **B.** 102 bugs; **C.** $8.00; **D.** 91 coins; **E.** 32 honks; **F.** 48 spoons of lemonade mix

**Page 88: A.** 6 toys; **B.** 3 papers; **C.** 6 cookies; **D.** 22 horses

**Page 89: A.** 4, 2; **B.** 7, 1; **C.** 2, 1; **D.** 6, 1

**Page 90: A.** 37 minutes; **B.** 9:00 P.M.; **C.** 7 minutes; **D.** 8:47 P.M.; **E.** 1 hour and 21 minutes; **F.** 3 hours

**Page 91: A.** $22.22; **B.** $4.27; **C.** $17.50; **D.** $34.00; **E.** $32.00; **F.** $12.00

**Page 92: A.** 20 minutes; **B.** 18 hours

**Summer Bridge Math** RB-904087 © Rainbow Bridge Publishing